MW00770009

SIGHING ON SUNDAY

40 Meditations for When Church Hurts

MEGAN HILL

P U B L I S H I N G

P.O. BOX 817 • PHILLIPSBURG • NEW JERSEY 08865-0817

Cover design by Jelena Mirkovic

Printed in the United States of America

Library of Congress Cataloging-in-Publication Data

Names: Hill, Megan, 1978- author.
Title: Sighing on Sunday : 40 meditations for when church hurts / Megan Hill.
Description: Phillipsburg : P&R Publishing Company, [2024] | Includes bibliographical references. | Summary: "Are your Sunday mornings more difficult than joyous? Forty thoughtful meditations on biblical truths encourage readers to understand the source of their struggle, express their sorrow, and take wise action"-- Provided by publisher.
Identifiers: LCCN 2023046894 | ISBN 9781629959849 (hardback) | ISBN 9781629959856 (epub)
Subjects: LCSH: Church attendance--Psychological aspects--Meditations. | Suffering--Biblical teaching--Meditations. | Consolation--Biblical teaching--Meditations.
Classification: LCC BV4523 .H549 2024 | DDC 262--dc23/eng/20240202
LC record available at https://lccn.loc.gov/2023046894

The LORD is near to the brokenhearted
and saves the crushed in spirit.
(Ps. 34:18)

CONTENTS

Contents

Why Should I Trust God When Church Hurts?

What Can I Do?

Why Should I Keep Showing Up?

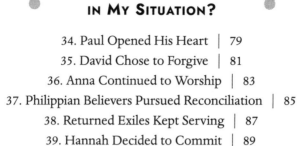

WHAT HAVE OTHERS DONE IN MY SITUATION?

INTRODUCTION

We sat in the car for nearly an hour. Outside the windows, we could see people gathering for a picnic in the backyard of a church member, but we didn't open the doors. Instead, I listened while the woman next to me, a member of my church, told me her story of past hurt.

That wasn't the first time I'd heard a church story like hers—of trust broken, friendships lost, and faith shaken—and it was far from the last.

More than forty years ago, I was born into a pastor's family. I napped on the church chairs on Sundays and stayed up late waiting for my dad to come home from long meetings. I'm thankful my parents always communicated to me that life in the church is fundamentally good. But that doesn't mean it's not also hard.

Over my lifetime, I've belonged to a variety of churches. And like anyone who has been in the church for more than a few Sundays, I've been hurt and I've walked with people who have been hurt. The churches I've belonged to have been good churches, churches that loved Christ and proclaimed his gospel. They've also been churches filled with not-yet-glorified saints and under attack from the enemy of God's people.

If you and I could sit together in a car outside a church picnic—watching everyone walk past with their casserole dishes and pitchers of iced tea—we could share our stories. But even without hearing yours (or being able to tell you the details of mine), I can guess the kinds of things we'd talk about.

We'd have stories about hurtful comments and thoughtless actions from other church members. We'd remember times when we were ignored and times when we were deliberately excluded. We'd grieve over pastors and elders who failed to shepherd our souls well. We'd recall friends who are no longer speaking to each other and angry words that can never be unsaid. We'd sigh thinking about ministries that bore little fruit and churches that ultimately shut their doors.

Perhaps we'd even talk about agonizing situations: pastors caught in moral failing, church splits, abuse, slander, financial wrongdoing, crimes committed in the steeple's shadow.

We'd confess to sometimes doubting God himself, questioning if he's really good and wondering if there's any hope for life in his church.

If we sat there for a while—long after the grills were fired up and the children began sneaking brownies from the edges of the platters—we could weep together. And then we could seek a balm for our hurts. We could turn together to the only source of comfort and hope: Jesus Christ as he is revealed in Scripture. And we could begin to apply healing medicine from the hand of that most tender Physician.

This book is born out of my own experiences in the church and out of hearing the experiences of others. But mostly it's born out of the comforts of Scripture. The Word of God alone supplies the unchanging truth and unfailing encouragement that hurting people desperately need, and each of the meditations in this book is designed to apply that precious balm to our wounds.

You'll notice this book is divided into six sections. In the first section ("What Is Happening?"), we'll see seven different kinds of hurt that believers experience in the church. We'll discover that the Bible doesn't ignore the reality of hurt in the covenant community; in fact, Scripture testifies that believers throughout history have experienced it. Next, we'll ask the question "Why Is Church So Hard?" and answer it by looking at some big truths about why hurt happens. Then we'll consider "Why Should I Trust God When Church Hurts?" and see how the character of our God can lead us to trust him in the midst of trials. The fourth section, "What Can I Do?," examines godly responses that we should have when we are hurt and warns against some common tactics of Satan that would draw us into deeper misery. Fifth, we'll turn our attention to Christ's relationship to the church and ask "Why Should I Keep Showing Up?" Finally, we'll consider the answer to the question, "What Have Others Done in My Situation?" and see how the people from the first section were able to flourish even after hurt.

Although it may feel right now like what you need is a quick solution, I'd encourage you to read this book from beginning to end, taking as much time as you need between meditations. To rightly understand hard situations, we need the whole scope of the Bible's testimony about things like sin's pervasiveness, God's character, and the church's value—even when those truths don't seem to fix our problems immediately. The God who made us and takes care of us has provided encouragements for us throughout his Word, and I don't want you to miss any of them.

This is a book you can read on your own, of course, but you may want to read it with a friend or a group of friends. Each meditation includes reflection questions that could facilitate discussion. As we noted earlier, most Christians who have spent time in the church have a story of hurt, and we can help one another best when we are all supplied with the Bible's healing balm.

I may not know the specifics of your hard church story, but I do know where to get help. Come and see.

WHAT IS HAPPENING?

I'm sorry you've had to pick up this book. If you're reading this, it's probably because your church is a hard place for you right now. Whatever the specific circumstance, I'm sure you're doing a lot of sighing, and maybe even weeping, on Sundays. An experience that's meant to be joyful—worshipping with the body of Christ—is now sad and difficult. And it has implications for every day of the week as you try to navigate damaged relationships and disappointed expectations. I'm sorry.

In these first seven meditations, we're going to answer the question "What Is Happening?" We'll consider seven types of hurt that happen in the church, and to do that, we'll look at seven different people (or groups of people) from Scripture who experienced hurt in the community of believers. Some of them are from the Old Testament, where God gathered his covenant people as the nation of Israel. Some of them are from the New Testament, where God gathered his covenant people as the church. All of them have been in a hard situation like the one where you are now.

As you read each meditation, I simply want you to notice that God does not ignore hurt in the church. In fact, he tenderly records each of these people's sorrows in his Word. I also want you to take comfort from the fact that you are not alone. The hard things that are happening to you have happened to God's people before you, and just as God was faithful to them, he will be faithful to you.

DAY 1

I'M BEING NEGLECTED

At my first defense no one came to stand by me,
but all deserted me. (2 Tim. 4:16)

The man shuffles toward the Roman magistrate in chains. This will be a hard day. He's innocent, but the political system is out for him, and he doubts he'll get a fair trial. He needs to defend himself, but he knows his critics are preparing their accusations. *Maybe*, he thinks, *someone is here to support me.* He scans the crowd, looking for a familiar face—another Christian with an encouraging smile or an outstretched hand. The members of the church knew he'd have his hearing today. They also knew how much he valued their relationship. He'd pastored and prayed for them for years; many of them came to faith because of his ministry. But as the man reaches the front, he realizes he will have to do this alone. Not a single church member showed up.

Today's verse may be the saddest sentence in all of Paul's writings. At the end of a long ministry to which he had dedicated his life, Paul sat in prison for the sake of Christ and because of his relationship to the church. Called to defend himself, though, he appeared alone.

It's painful to witness the depths of Paul's sadness here. "No one" came with him. "All" abandoned him. And the Christians in Rome didn't simply forget—that would be hurtful enough—but they deliberately chose not to accompany Paul; they "deserted" him. Like the disciples who fled on the night of Jesus's crucifixion, the members of the church looked out for themselves and decided not to look out for Paul.

Perhaps that's been your experience too. Maybe church members don't notice the hard time you are going through, maybe they haven't

3

prayed for you or checked on you, or maybe nobody recognizes your gifts or welcomes you into the life of the church. Maybe you've been serving and everyone takes it for granted, or maybe you've been struggling and the congregation gave up helping when your troubles began to drag on.

Dear Christian, this is hard. You may feel entirely ignored, but please know you are not. The Lord saw Paul, and he sees you: "No one came to stand by me," Paul wrote, ". . . but the Lord stood by me" (2 Tim. 4:16, 17).

> **Read.** Read Acts 6:1–7 and Galatians 2:11–14. Who is being neglected in each of these accounts? What were the reasons for the neglect? What was the resolution? How could it help you to know that neglect in the church is not new and that neglect has various causes? How does it encourage you to know that God addresses neglect?
>
> **Reflect.** A Lifeway Research study reported that people's reasons for leaving church are often related to neglect. Respondents said "church members . . . 'were judgmental of others' (17 percent) [and] 'the church was run by a clique that discouraged involvement' (12 percent)." Additionally, when the respondents stopped going to church, "Sixteen percent said 'nobody contacted me after I left' and another 16 percent said 'nobody seemed to care that I left.'" Why do you think being neglected in the church is so hurtful?
>
> **Pray.** Tell the Lord about a time when you've been neglected in the church. Ask him to draw near to you as the God who cares for the weak and rescues the one who "has no helper" (Ps. 72:12). Thank him for having his eyes toward you and his ears toward your cry (Ps. 34:15).

DAY 2

I'M BEING SINNED AGAINST

For it is not an enemy who taunts me. . . . But it is you,
a man, my equal, my companion, my familiar friend.
We used to take sweet counsel together; within God's
house we walked in the throng. (Ps. 55:12–14)

David was in a hard place. He was restless, he moaned, he trembled, he prayed. His days held anguish, terror, and horror. He wanted to run away. But, unlike difficult situations David describes in other psalms, this was different. This time, David's oppressor wasn't a pagan army coming against him from the outside. His oppressor was his friend. And not just any friend—a close friend, a friend who regularly worshipped with him in God's house.

The companion who used to go up to the temple with David didn't even come against him with fist or voice raised. That, at least, would have been obvious to everyone. Instead, David's friend set out to destroy him with sneaky words. He spoke his lies smoothly and softly—no one would have known what he was up to—but "war was in his heart" (v. 21).

His betrayal was so hurtful that David says he'd rather face an army. It's hard to be taunted by an enemy, but it's what David expected, so it was bearable. It's not easy to hear insults from an adversary, but at least David had the option to walk away (v. 12). But when it's a fellow-worshipper who sins against you? David says that's when he was completely overwhelmed.

Maybe you too have been deliberately sinned against by someone in your congregation. Maybe you've experienced unkindness, gossip, partiality, and slander. Maybe you've even been the victim of bullying or abuse. Maybe you can say, as David did in another psalm, "Even

5

my close friend in whom I trusted, who ate my bread, has lifted his heel against me" (Ps. 41:9).

This hurts—perhaps more than being openly attacked by unbelievers—because our fellow church members profess to be changed by Christ and believe his gospel. When they sin against us, their speech may sound graceful, but their actions violate their covenant with God and his people (Ps. 55:20).

In response to his troubles, David's instinct was to "wander far away" and to "lodge in the wilderness" (v. 7). Joining "the throng" (v. 14) in God's house is often the last thing you want to do when it's a place where you've been mistreated like David was. The wilderness may be harsh and lonely, you think, but at least nobody can hurt you there.

But David found two comforts in his distress: the Lord's tender care for his people (v. 22) and the Lord's certain justice for wrongdoers (v. 23). Dear Christian, the Lord looks on you with love and will deal with every sin committed against you. Either those sins were laid on Christ and paid for at the cross, or they will be judged by God on the last day. Your hurt has not been forgotten.

Read. Read 2 Samuel 16:5–14. List the ways Shimei sinned against David; if you can, use biblical terms for those sins. What was Abishai's instinct? Can you relate? List the reasons David gives for overlooking Shimei's attack. Can you apply any of those reasons to your own situation? Did ignoring Shimei seem to resolve the situation (see vv. 13–14)? How does the frankness of this story encourage you in your experience of hurt?

Reflect. Do you agree with David's assessment that it's easier to be hurt by a known enemy than to be hurt by a friend and fellow believer? Why is hurt from a Christian friend so damaging?

Pray. Tell the Lord about the sins committed against you. If you can, use biblical terms for those sins. Using the words of Psalm 55, ask God to sustain you (v. 18) and to give you justice (v. 19). Ask him to help you trust him (v. 23).

DAY 3

I'M ENDURING DIFFICULT PERSONAL CIRCUMSTANCES

And there was a prophetess, Anna, the daughter of Phanuel, of the tribe of Asher. She was advanced in years, having lived with her husband seven years from when she was a virgin, and then as a widow until she was eighty-four. She did not depart from the temple, worshiping with fasting and prayer night and day. (Luke 2:36–37)

The old woman hobbled across the temple courtyard, a singular figure in a crowd of families. She was a prophetess from the tribe of Asher—one of the so-called "lost tribes" of Israel's northern kingdom that had rebelled with Jeroboam and then been conquered by Assyria and sent into exile (1 Kings 12:16–21). Her ancestors had been so scattered that most people believed the family line extinct. What's more, the woman had no immediate family. Her husband had died long ago, and, if she had children, they weren't around. She was also "advanced in years." She had witnessed the siege of her city and the conquest of the Romans; now, her body was deteriorating and the grave waited. And if all this weren't hard enough, she was financially vulnerable—an elderly widow in a society without safety nets, dependent on others' generosity to provide for her needs.

Today's verse paints a picture of a woman who came to worship bearing the weight of personal hardship. Anna sang psalms, listened to Scripture, and offered prayers alongside people who had social connections, spouses, children, money, and the vigor of youth. But Anna had none of those. Over her lifetime, Anna had accumulated many reasons to feel out of place in the congregation.

7

The crowds in the temple may have been oblivious to Anna's difficulties, but the Bible doesn't hurry past her losses. The Lord gives tender attention to the personal circumstances that made it hard for Anna to show up to worship, day after day, for decades.

Maybe you can relate to Anna. Sometimes church hurts not because of the church, but because circumstances in our lives increase the difficulty of being with God's people. An unbelieving spouse or unwanted singleness can provoke grief—especially when we see happy families in other pews. Illness or disability can make participating in worship difficult. Financial difficulties or job loss can convince us we don't belong with people who seem to have their lives together.

Anna spent decades going to worship alone, with a failing body, lacking financial security. The Lord knew this, and he graciously placed her in the right place at the right time to welcome the Messiah (v. 38). In answer to her prayers of many years, the Lord allowed her to see Jesus.

Dear Christian, be encouraged. If Christ met Anna in her hardship, he will meet you in yours.

Read. Read Luke 8:42–48. What was the woman's situation? What do you think her decision to approach Jesus from behind (v. 44) and to remain hidden (v. 47) tells us about how she was feeling? If neither the disciples nor the people in the crowd noticed her (v. 45), what does that tell us about her relationship to Jesus's followers? How does Jesus respond to her? How can this story encourage you when you come burdened to church?

Reflect. How do personal trials make it difficult to come to worship? Why is it often hard to be around people who have blessings that we do not?

Pray. Tell the Lord about your circumstances. Ask him to help you in your troubles (Ps. 46:1). Thank him for promising to be "near to the brokenhearted and [to save] the crushed in spirit" (Ps. 34:18).

DAY 4

I'M OBSERVING CONGREGATIONAL CONFLICT

I entreat Euodia and I entreat Syntyche to agree in the Lord. (Phil. 4:2)

The congregation at Philippi had obviously been transformed by Christ (Phil. 1:6). They abounded in love (1:8–10). They were consistently obedient to the Lord (2:12). They were generous, supporting the work of missions whenever they had opportunity (4:10–18). The apostle Paul delighted in them (1:3–5). Philippi was the kind of church anyone would have been happy to join, and everyone would have encouraged their friends to visit.

Except for one thing. The congregation at Philippi had a problem. For most of them, it wasn't a personal problem, but it was troubling nevertheless. Two of their members, Euodia and Syntyche, were locked in a feud, and everyone knew it. Scripture doesn't tell us what the subject of their disagreement was, but the fact that Paul urges them to agree seems to indicate the conflict was a petty one—or at least one with an obvious right answer.

It may have started over something trivial, but Paul's specific attention to it probably means the ongoing conflict was upsetting and wearing down the congregation. When the church gathered for worship or fellowship, they were aware of the tension. Life with irritable people is "a continual dripping of rain" (Prov. 19:13), and Paul's earlier instructions to "do all things without grumbling or disputing" (Phil. 2:14) may hint that Euodia and Syntyche's quarrelsomeness was drawing others into habitual strife.

Maybe in your church too a conflict is ripping people apart. The conflict could involve church members or elders. It could be a matter between two individuals or between entire segments of the congregation. It could have begun over a petty matter of personal preference or over a strongly held theological conviction. It may even be a necessary confrontation (see, for example, Gal. 2:11–12). But, whatever its dimensions, church conflict is difficult to witness. People may even have left the church as a result, and you may be grieving departed friends while navigating the minefield that remains.

The New Testament Epistles, written to first-century churches, include both reports of quarreling (see 1 Cor. 1:11; James 4:1) and warnings against quarreling (see 2 Tim. 2:23; Titus 3:9), demonstrating that Philippi was not the only congregation with a conflict problem. Although we ought to "be at peace with one another" (Mark 9:50) in the church, we too often devolve into arguments.

Dear Christian, the Lord includes this story of Euodia and Syntyche in his Word to remind us that any church can have conflict and that he is intimately involved in dealing with it when it arises.

Read. Read Numbers 12:1–16. How did Miriam and Aaron create conflict with Moses? What effect do you think this had in the congregation of Israel? What does verse 2 ("And the LORD heard it") tell you about the Lord's concern for his people when there is conflict? How did the Lord respond to the conflict? How does this story encourage you to know that the Lord won't ignore the conflict in your church?

Reflect. We expect conflict among unbelievers, but it can catch us by surprise when it happens in the church. Why is church conflict so distressing? What effects does it have on the participants who start it, the congregation members who observe it, and the unbelievers who may hear of it?

Pray. Tell the Lord about the conflict in your church. Lament the bad effects it has had on everyone connected to it. Ask him to bless your congregation with unity (Ps. 133).

DAY 5

I'M GRIEVING CHANGES

But many of the priests and Levites and heads of fathers' houses,
old men who had seen the first house, wept with a loud voice when
they saw the foundation of this house being laid. (Ezra 3:12)

The old men may have had aging bodies, but their minds were
sharp and their hearts still sought the Lord. They could remember
Solomon's temple (1 Kings 6:1–8:11) as though they had walked
through it yesterday. Walls lined with cedar, floors covered in cypress,
everything overlaid in gold. Carvings of cherubim and gourds and
lions and palm trees and flowers. And, most precious of all, the ark
of the Lord that had gone with God's people since their exodus from
Egypt. Everyone who remembered it agreed it was a magnificent
temple, filled with the Lord's presence.

But that temple was gone—destroyed by the Babylonians
decades ago—and in its place was the bare foundation of a new
temple. The old men could already tell this temple wouldn't compare
with the one they remembered from childhood. God's people no
longer had Solomon's wealth or his workforce. They labored under
threats from their enemies. And, worst of all, they no longer had
the ark. As the old men looked at the fresh foundation, they could
only weep.

Maybe you too have experienced unwanted changes in the place
where you worship. Perhaps a pastoral transition or dwindling membership has left you longing for past days when your church was
thriving and even unbelievers in the community could see how well
it was doing. Or maybe your church has changed its practice—using
different music in worship, abandoning its women's ministry, or
closing the doors on a long-standing community outreach. Maybe

11

programs you've invested in for years have ceased to exist because no one is interested in continuing them.

It might even feel like you are the only one who mourns the change. Some of the returned exiles wept, but others "shouted aloud for joy" (Ezra 3:12) and "the people could not distinguish the sound of the joyful shout from the sound of the people's weeping, for the people shouted with a great shout" (v. 13). Your sorrow over what has been lost may not be acknowledged in your congregation. Maybe others don't remember the past, or maybe they don't care. Your heart is broken, but nobody hears the sound of your weeping.

The verses of Ezra 3 assure us that the Lord knows the hurt when our labors in the church seem to come to nothing and when the church we remember is not the church we have today. The second temple was a sign of the Lord's continued faithfulness to his people, but he doesn't tell its story without acknowledging the old men's grief. And even when the Israelites couldn't distinguish the sound of weeping, the Lord recorded it in his book.

Dear weeping Christian, seek comfort from the Lord: "You have kept count of my tossings; put my tears in your bottle. Are they not in your book?" (Ps. 56:8).

Read. Read Psalm 46. List the images the psalmist uses for his experience of turmoil and change. Would you describe your experiences in similar ways? List the images the psalmist uses for God's unchanging presence. How is this a comfort to you in times of upheaval? Who dwells in "the city of God" (v. 4)? How does this description give you hope for Christ's church?

Reflect. Why is change hard? Why are changes in the church especially painful?

Pray. Tell the Lord your sorrow over changes in your church. Thank him for the good things he has done in your church in the past. Ask him to help you trust him for the future: "whoever has despised the day of small things shall rejoice" (Zech. 4:10).

I'M BEING LED BY
SINFUL SHEPHERDS

And Eli said to her, "How long will you go on being drunk?
Put your wine away from you." (1 Sam. 1:14)

As much as Hannah loved the Lord, going to worship was difficult. Her great desire was to have a child, and the Lord had closed her womb. Her husband's other wife had children, though, and she provoked Hannah about it. Every year, when Hannah went to the place of worship, her pilgrimage ended in tears (1 Sam. 1:1–7). One day, she took her sorrow into the temple at Shiloh and poured out her heart before the Lord—her husband's choice to take another wife, her barren womb, her rival's unkindness, her husband's assumption that everything should be fine—surely all of it came out. And in the middle of her prayer, Eli the high priest called out to her from his seat by the door and accused her of being a drunkard.

Eli's failures as a spiritual shepherd were legion. Hannah had gone "year by year" (v. 7) to Shiloh, and yet Eli didn't recognize her, let alone have any knowledge of her ongoing grief. Hannah came before the Lord in faith, and yet Eli characterized her prayer as sin-soaked rambling. Hannah was in need—in "great anxiety and vexation" (v. 16)—and yet Eli met her with a sharp rebuke.

Eli's conduct toward the other worshippers wasn't much better than his treatment of Hannah. He honored his sons above the Lord and with disregard for the Lord's people (2:29). He "kept hearing" how his sons took the people's offerings for themselves and how they slept with the women who served in the tent of meeting, but Scripture only records one ineffective rebuke from him (2:22–25).

While his flock suffered, Eli largely did nothing. He was a weak and sinful shepherd.

Maybe you too have had pastors and elders who didn't listen to you, neglected to care for you, taught error, acted selfishly, or even abused you. Or perhaps they failed your whole church by falling into scandalous sin. Maybe the leaders you trusted to point you to Christ were actually "worthless men" who "did not know the Lord" (2:12). Or they may have been genuine believers who were not qualified to be elders in the first place (Titus 1:5–9; 1 Tim. 3:1–7; 1 Peter 5:1–4) and did much harm by taking an office they couldn't uphold.

Hannah's story reminds us that the Lord sees the pain of having shepherds who are not shepherds in the likeness of Christ. When Hannah was in distress, "the LORD remembered her" (1 Sam. 1:19). Her whole story—including her treatment at the hands of a sinful shepherd—was known to the Lord.

Dear Christian, just as the Lord remembered Hannah, he remembers you.

Read. Read Ezekiel 34:1–16. What charges does the Lord bring against the shepherds of Israel? What does the Lord say he will do because of their sins? Does it comfort you to know the Lord sees and brings justice against sinful shepherds? Why? Who is the Good Shepherd the Lord promises (see John 10:11)? List the things the Lord promises to do as the Good Shepherd. Does it encourage you to know the Lord cares for you in these ways? Why?

Reflect. The Bible's repeated condemnations of hypocrites and warnings against false teachers make it clear that these are real problems for the church. Why are wolves in sheep's clothing (Matt. 7:15) so dangerous?

Pray. Tell the Lord how you have been hurt by someone who was meant to shepherd your soul. Ask the Lord to be the Good Shepherd to you. Ask him to seek you, rescue you, gather you, feed you, strengthen you, heal you, and give you rest (Ezek. 34:11–16).

DAY 7

I'M BEING REJECTED

[Jesus] came to his own, and his own people
did not receive him. (John 1:11)

It had been three long years. After his baptism, Jesus had spent forty days in the wilderness, fasting and being tempted by the devil (Luke 4:1–13). And as soon as he returned, he faced more trouble. The citizens of his hometown rejected him—even trying to throw him off a cliff—because he was nothing special in their eyes and they didn't want to hear what he had to say (Luke 4:16, 22–30). The scribes and Pharisees looked for reasons to accuse him (Luke 6:7), the people said he was an agent of Satan (Luke 11:15), a government official beheaded his forerunner in ministry (Matt. 14:3–11), and crowds of people followed him just to see what miracle he would do next (Luke 11:16, 29). At the end, the chief priests, the elders, and the high priest concocted a secret plot to arrest and kill him (Matt. 26:3–4).

Wherever Jesus went, he had enemies. But he also had friends. A group of men and women—a small congregation of believers—traveled with him, received his teaching, and provided for his needs (Luke 8:1–3). Even when the Pharisees made accusations and the crowds gathered looking for a spectacle, Jesus's friends loved him and believed he was who he said he was (John 16:27). For three years, they remained by his side.

Until they didn't.

On the night of his arrest, "all the disciples left him and fled" (Matt. 26:56). During the most difficult hours of his life, Jesus was abandoned, betrayed, and rejected *by his friends* (Matt. 26:47–50, 56, 69–75). One of his closest disciples even swore up and down that he wasn't a friend of Jesus at all. With a terse sentence in a dark

15

courtyard, Peter denied the One who was at that moment laying down his life for him: "I do not know the man" (Matt. 26:72, 74).

For the past six days, we have looked at Old and New Testament believers who were hurt and hurting in the assembly of worshippers. Their examples encourage us that the Lord sees hurt in the church, and he doesn't minimize it or cover it up. But the Lord doesn't simply observe his people's hurt. He entered into it. The eternal Son took on human flesh and came to earth, "and his own people did not receive him" (John 1:11). He loved the church (Eph. 5:25), and yet he was "despised and rejected . . . a man of sorrows and acquainted with grief" (Isa. 53:3). In his life and on the cross, Jesus the sinless God-man experienced deeper hurt than any person ever has. And he did it for our sake (vv. 4–6).

Dear Christian, turn to Jesus.

Read. Read Isaiah 53, one of the great Old Testament prophesies of the coming Messiah. What images does Isaiah use to describe Jesus's hurt and rejection? Can you relate? How do Christ's sufferings on your behalf comfort you?

Reflect. The account of Jesus's last days includes numerous rejections (see Matt. 26). Some came from people who didn't profess love for Jesus. Others came from Jesus's friends. As Christians, we can face rejection in both the world and the church. In what ways have you experienced rejection among believers? Why is it especially hurtful?

Pray. Thank the Lord for sending Jesus to enter into suffering so our sins could be forgiven. Praise him because "he has not despised or abhorred the affliction of the afflicted, and he has not hidden his face from him, but has heard, when he cried to him" (Ps. 22:24).

WHY IS CHURCH
SO HARD?

In this section, we'll answer the question "Why Is Church So Hard?" There are only four fundamental reasons for hurt in the church: the fall's effects, Satan's schemes, human weakness, and human sin. Your hurt may be caused by just one of these factors, or, more likely, a few of them are each contributing in different ways.

As you read each meditation, I want to help you categorize and understand what lies behind your hurt. In my own life, I've found it immensely helpful to distinguish which hard situations are deliberately orchestrated and which are simply the repercussions of a broken world, which actions are malicious and which may arise from someone's frailty. This shines light in hurt's darkness and enables me to begin to think clearly about how to respond. In any difficult situation, it's also helpful to remember that there's more going on than we can perceive with our physical senses—there are spiritual forces at work that affect every aspect of life in the church.

The four realities in this section are the same ones that have troubled believers since the garden of Eden. And for generations, believers have looked in hope to the Messiah, the one who conquers sin and Satan and who makes all things new. Your hurt has a cause, and Jesus *will* triumph over it.

DAY 8

WE LIVE IN A FALLEN WORLD

For we know that the whole creation has been groaning together in the
pains of childbirth until now. And not only the creation, but we ourselves,
who have the firstfruits of the Spirit, groan inwardly as we wait eagerly
for adoption as sons, the redemption of our bodies. (Rom. 8:22–23)

The greatest disaster in the history of the world happened right at
its very beginning. In the garden, Adam and Eve had everything they
could need: beautiful surroundings, delicious food, meaningful work,
ideal companionship, and an intimate relationship with God (Gen. 2).
Then they sinned. Adam and Eve ate the fruit God commanded
them not to eat, and nothing in the world has been the same since.

Because of Adam's fall, every human is born with a sinful nature,
is under God's wrath and curse, and is unable to save him or herself.
The fall also has implications for creation in general. The penalty
for Adam's sin includes pain, discord, hardship, obstacles, fruitless-
ness, disappointment, and death (Gen. 3:16–19). Because of the fall,
nothing on earth works as smoothly as it did at creation. As today's
verses remind us, the whole world is groaning.

In the church we experience the effects of the fall. Growth can
be slow, financial troubles loom, buildings are inadequate (or not to
be had), programs never get off the ground, church members get
sick or move away or die, and all our sweat on the church's behalf
doesn't seem to produce much yield. Some of these hardships may
be the direct result of a particular person's sin, but often they are
simply the features of life after Eden.

We usually accept the fact that projects in our workplaces sometimes don't succeed and that our homes fill with dust as soon as
we've cleaned them, but we don't always acknowledge that life in the

church inevitably includes ordinary difficulties and discouragements. We'd like to think every good effort will always advance smoothly in God's kingdom, but even the church has to balance the budget and reschedule events. Sometimes the problems we face on Sundays are not because we are in church but because we are in a fallen world.

Today's verses don't leave us without hope, however. As Paul reminds us, creation's groaning has an end in view. Like childbirth—which is painful for a time but results in the blessing of new life—our groaning under failed ministries and dwindling resources should focus us on a joyful future. One day soon, Christ will fully and finally redeem this world from the curse and usher in a new creation. For those who look to him in faith, the discouragements of earthly church life will pass away, and we "shall obtain gladness and joy, and sorrow and sighing shall flee away" (Isa. 35:10).

> **Read.** Read Isaiah 35. List the images that illustrate the struggles God's people face in a fallen world. How are each of those difficulties reversed in the new creation Isaiah describes? As a result of the fall, what specific difficulties have come on your church? Imagine how each of those will be restored in eternity.
>
> **Reflect.** When we are discouraged or hurting, we can be quick to assume our struggles in the church are unique to the church. Why is it helpful to remember that the fall of Adam has implications for all of creation?
>
> **Pray.** Lament to the Lord the effects of the fall on your church. Thank him for sending Christ into the world. Praise him for promising to bring a new heaven and a new earth.

DAY 9

SATAN HATES THE CHURCH

Your adversary the devil prowls around like a roaring lion,
seeking someone to devour. Resist him, firm in your faith,
knowing that the same kinds of suffering are being experienced
by your brotherhood throughout the world. (1 Peter 5:8–9)

The churches in first-century Asia were struggling. Between them, the seven congregations had to contend with false teachers, poverty, slander, persecution, sexual immorality, and spiritual lethargy (see Rev. 1–3). To help them understand their situation, the Lord gave John a vision. In it, a great red dragon—"with seven heads and ten horns"—mounts an epic attack against a woman and her male child (Rev. 12:3). Eventually, the dragon is thrown down to earth. This signals his ultimate defeat, but it also makes him formidable because he has nothing to lose and he knows "his time is short" (v. 12). Furious with his situation, the soon-to-be-destroyed dragon turns against all the children of the woman and goes off to make war on them.

Who are those children? They are "those who keep the commandments of God and hold to the testimony of Jesus" (v. 17). And who is the dragon? He is "that ancient serpent, who is called the devil and Satan" (v. 9).

Sometimes finding an explanation for our church hurt requires us to pull back the curtain on the spiritual realm. And there we see that the dragon is out to get us.

Today's verses call the Evil One "a roaring lion," and opposing the church is one of his primary activities. He is our "adversary," he "prowls," and he is "seeking someone to devour." When church hurts, we should not be blind to the possibility that it is Satan's doing. Because he hates Christ, the Evil One uses every tool at his disposal to damage, persecute, and destroy Christ's church. He seeks to spread lies (John 8:44), confuse our doctrine (2 Cor. 11:3), separate us from Christ (Rom. 8:38–39), keep us from understanding the preaching of the Word (Matt. 13:19), exploit our anger for his own ends (Eph. 4:26–27), stir up controversy in the church (2 Tim. 2:23–26), prevent gospel workers from ministry (1 Thess. 2:17–18), magnify offenses in order to cause us to sin (2 Cor. 2:10–11), ensnare vulnerable Christians (1 Tim. 5:11–15), take down new believers (1 Tim. 3:6), and cause church members to fail to love each other (1 John 3:10). When we are hurt in the church, we can remember that the source of our hurt is often the Evil One who hates "the brotherhood throughout the world."

Perhaps surprisingly, this truth can also be a comfort. We are not alone. The same attacks that come against us also come against our brothers and sisters in all times and places. And take heart: "He who is in you is greater than he who is in the world" (1 John 4:4).

Read. Read Acts 4:32–5:11. How does Luke describe the church in Acts 4:32–37? How does this contrast with the story in 5:1–11? To what does Peter attribute Ananias and Sapphira's deceitful and self-serving behavior? What effect did Satan's act have on the whole congregation? In what additional ways do you think the believers in that church may have been hurt by the Evil One's ploy?

Reflect. Why are we often quick to look for temporal explanations and slow to look for spiritual ones? Why is it important to acknowledge the possibility that Satan is at work in our church situation?

Pray. Tell the Lord the ways you see Satan attacking your church. Ask him to have mercy: "Do not lead us into temptation, but deliver us from the evil one" (Matt. 6:13 NKJV).

DAY 10

PEOPLE ARE WEAK

*And we urge you, brothers and sisters, admonish the idle, encourage the
fainthearted, help the weak, be patient with them all. (1 Thess. 5:14)*

On the night of his betrayal, Jesus took his disciples—the small congregation who had supported him in his ministry—to Gethsemane.
There he selected three of his dearest friends and asked them to pray
for him while he withdrew to pray alone (Matt. 26:36–39). After an
hour, he returned to the group to find them sleeping. And even after
he woke them, they fell asleep twice more (vv. 40–45). When he was
in great distress, Jesus's fellow-worshippers repeatedly failed to care
for him. Confronting their inertia, though, he diagnosed not malice
but frailty: "The spirit indeed is willing, but the flesh is weak" (v. 41).

Sometimes people who hurt us in the church do so out of weakness. As we saw on day 8, we are fallen creatures in a fallen world, and
the effects of the curse often hamper our best intentions. In today's
verse, Paul writes to the church at Thessalonica and acknowledges
that the church is full of frail people. In every congregation, there
are people who sometimes neglect to act ("the idle"), people whose
fears and doubts cripple them ("the fainthearted"), and people whose
abilities are limited ("the weak"). These vulnerabilities can be complicated by personal sin, but they trace their roots back to the fall's
lingering effects on every human. Knowing this, Paul doesn't urge a
swift rebuke. He urges patience.

Sometimes people in the church act the way they do because
they are limited by time or ability, because they lack maturity or
knowledge, or because they are beset by physical or mental illness.
A congregation member with chronic disease may want to help but
be unable to commit in advance. A new believer may quote Bible

verses at you but lack the wisdom to offer comfort. These are the same kinds of struggles that have affected humans since the fall of Adam. Paul loved the Galatian church, but his "bodily ailment" was "a trial" to them (Gal. 4:13–14). Nathanael was committed to being honest, but his impulsive words were insulting (John 1:45–51). Apollos was zealous, but he was ignorant and taught incorrectly at first (Acts 18:24–28). Timothy, Titus, John, and others wanted to minister to the saints, but they could only "do [their] best" and wait for an opportunity (2 Tim. 4:9, 21; see also 1 Tim. 3:14; Titus 3:12; 2 John 1:12; 1 Cor. 16:12).

When people fail to care for us in the church, it hurts. They may be unavailable in our time of need, or their words and actions may be eager but ill-considered. To understand what's happening, we can remember that they—like all of us—are weak. This can give us sympathy for them. We can ask for the Spirit's help to be patient, recognizing that God has been patient with us in our weaknesses too (Ps. 103:13–14).

> **Read.** Read 1 Corinthians 12:12–26. Paul says the church is like a body: it has many parts, and every part is necessary. How are we connected in the church? What does Paul say about the weak parts? Why might that be surprising?
>
> **Reflect.** It's easy to look at people's actions and assume that what they did was exactly what they intended to do. When they hurt us, then, we often suppose that they wanted to hurt us. How can remembering that we are all weak reshape the way we view others' words and actions?
>
> **Pray.** Tell the Lord how you have been hurt by weak people. Confess your own weakness in loving others well. As you think ahead to interactions with church members, ask him to help you to "be patient with them all."

DAY 11

PEOPLE SIN

What causes quarrels and what causes fights among you? Is it not
this, that your passions are at war within you? (James 4:1)

When you first became a Christian, you may have thought the
church was filled with people who were nearly perfect. You may
have assumed that they'd always worship wholeheartedly, treat one
another kindly, and reach out to unbelievers boldly. It probably didn't
take too many Sundays for you to realize it's more complicated
than that.

The New Testament is honest about problems in the church. In
today's verse, James addresses the first-century congregations and
diagnoses the source of their conflicts. The reason you can't get
along and you keep hurting each other, James writes, is because,
even though you've been redeemed, you still have sin in your hearts.
Although we might like to think people in the church would always
act in holy ways, the testimony of Scripture is that believers struggle
against sin. In Paul's first letter to the church at Corinth, for example,
he declared two seemingly contradictory truths: the believers were
saints (1 Cor. 1:2), and the believers were sinners (15:34).

When Christ died on the cross, he paid sin's penalty and he broke
sin's power. Christ gives us new hearts and his indwelling Spirit, so
we can say no to sin and yes to righteousness. And yet, in this life,
we still battle against sin and frequently fall into it (see Rom. 6–7).

All around us, our fellow church members are caught in what
James calls a "war." People know they should do one thing, but they
often give in to sin and do the opposite. And sin in Christians' hearts
leads to hurt in their churches: "You desire and do not have, so you mur-
der. You covet and cannot obtain, so you fight and quarrel" (James 4:2).

When we experience sin in the church, we should be grieved, but we shouldn't be surprised.

Being sinned against in the church can feel very personal, but understanding the reality and nature of sin can allow you to see the situation more clearly. The believer who sinned against you has a major conflict raging in his or her own heart (as you do in yours); in the moment of sinning, that Christian lost a skirmish against evil "passions" that were "at war" within.

When we come to church, we are not entering a downtown showroom but a battlefield hospital—an institution designed by God to diagnose and cut out the cancer of sin and to remake all of us in the image of the Son. As any seriously ill person can tell you, living as a patient among other patients isn't easy; in fact, it's often extremely painful. But, like hospitals, churches are designed for our healing.

Read. Read 1 Corinthians 3:1–4; 5:1–2; 6:1–8; 11:17–22. These passages mention just some of the sins that plagued the church at Corinth. Make a list of the ones you noticed. Does it surprise you that these sins were present in the church? Why or why not? How is the Bible's honesty about these sins—and Paul's efforts to address them—a comfort to you?

Reflect. In the reflection for day 10, we saw that recognizing other Christians' weakness can help us understand that their actions don't necessarily align with their intentions. How can recognizing other believers' ongoing battle with sin similarly help us understand their conduct?

Pray. Lament to God the effects of sin in your church. Confess to him ways you have sinned against others. Ask him to make your church a place that confronts sin and encourages righteousness. Praise him as the God who "forgiv[es] iniquity and transgression and sin, but who will by no means clear the guilty" (Ex. 34:7).

WHY SHOULD I TRUST GOD WHEN CHURCH HURTS?

In the midst of your hard situation, you may have said to your-self, *I know I should trust God*. If you have, that's good. I'm glad you're encouraging your soul to take refuge in the Lord. But a self-exhortation like that can feel pretty hollow if you aren't really sure *why* you ought to trust him. And to know why you should trust God, you have to know who God is.

In the next set of meditations, we'll answer the question, "Why Should I Trust God When Church Hurts?" To do that, we'll look at four truths about who God is, and we'll let them give us good reason to rely on him. God is sovereign, powerful, unchanging, and loving. Because of this, we can come to him with all our sighs and cast on him all our cares. These truths also counter the hurtful realities we saw in the last section. Church hurts because of the effects of the fall, but God is sovereign over his whole creation. Church hurts because Satan wants to destroy us, but God is all-powerful. Church hurts because people fail, but God is perfectly consistent—always acting according to his holy character. Church hurts because people sin against us, but God is loving all the time.

As you read, I want to invite you to meditate on your God. I know you're hurt. Let the Lord's gracious character be a balm to your wounds. He is God and there is no other, and he alone is worthy of your trust.

DAY 12

GOD IS SOVEREIGN

Am I in the place of God? . . . You meant evil against
me, but God meant it for good. (Gen. 50:19, 20)

Joseph's life in the covenant community appeared to be a series of
undeserved setbacks and senseless injustices. When he was a teenager,
Joseph's brothers hated him and were jealous of him (Gen. 37:2–11).
Later, they assaulted him and sold him into slavery among the pagans,
effectively banishing him from God's people and cutting him off
from fellowship and worship (vv. 18–28). Because of this, Joseph
lived and worked among godless people who mistreated him even
further (Gen. 39–40).

After many years, the brothers came to Joseph, looking for his
help and, ultimately, for his forgiveness (Gen. 43–45; 50:15–21). Joseph's
words in today's verses reveal the truth that sustained him: "God
meant it for good." Tumbled in the relentless waves of sin that came
against him, Joseph could only rest on God's purposeful sovereignty.

Like Joseph, when we are hurt by another believer's actions or
suffer the effects of others' sin, it can seem like our plans for our lives
have come crashing down around us. Difficulty, disappointment, and
mistreatment in the church all make us feel out of control. In those
seasons, why should we trust God? Joseph reminds us that we can
find security in God's unfailing purposes.

In Psalm 33, the psalmist tells us that God's rule is over all he
has made: the earth fears him and the world's citizens should be in
awe of him (v. 8). Whatever he determines to do he does (v. 9), and
nothing and no one can stand in his way (v. 10). What's more, his
sovereign will never falters but remains steadfast from one genera-
tion to another (v. 11).

We may not understand why a beloved church member has to move away or why financial difficulties are forcing the church to let a dear pastor go. We can't make sense out of the seemingly petty miscommunication that led to a church split or the reasons that our adult children stopped attending. We aren't able to bring any good from our hurt and disappointment. But the Lord can.

When circumstances in the church make us feel out of control, we know the One who is in control. God rules over every detail of his creation and executes his plans perfectly. His good purposes are being accomplished even now. This means that we can trust him with every situation—even the hard ones. Our Lord's counsel stands forever.

> **Read.** Read 1 Peter 1:6–7. What is troubling these churches? How does it encourage you to know that trials are "for a little while" and "if necessary"? What does Peter say are God's purposes in trials?
>
> **Reflect.** John Piper said, "God is always doing 10,000 things in your life, and you may be aware of 3 of them."[1] When church hurts, how does it encourage you to remember that God has purposes in your life (and in the lives of your fellow church members) that you don't even know about?
>
> **Pray.** Cry out to the Lord in your hurt and disappointment. Ask him to remind you of his sovereign care over all he has made. Ask him to remind you of his sovereign care for you in the past. Ask him to send his Spirit to help you to trust his sovereign purposes now. Praise him that he designs your hard circumstances to display "the tested genuineness of your faith—more precious than gold that perishes" (1 Peter 1:7).

DAY 13

GOD IS POWERFUL

Who is like you, O LORD, among the gods? Who is like you, majestic in holiness, awesome in glorious deeds, doing wonders? You stretched out your right hand; the earth swallowed them. You have led in your steadfast love the people whom you have redeemed; you have guided them by your strength to your holy abode. (Ex. 15:11–13)

The congregation of Israel was in trouble. For generations, they had been oppressed. By government order, the Egyptians beat the Israelites, killed their infant sons, and "made their lives bitter" (Ex. 1:14). Faced with persecution from the outside, some Israelites courageously united in their refusal to act wickedly (vv. 15–22), but others allowed internal conflicts to divide them (2:11–14). During "those many days," the congregation cried out to God for help (v. 23). Then, Moses wrote, "God saw the people of Israel—and God knew" (v. 25).

When our own congregations are in trouble—whether through outside attacks or internal strife—we feel vulnerable. We know we can't solve the complex problems that make our church lives bitter. On our own, we're powerless to reclaim departing church members, reignite the faith of the lukewarm, reconcile the disagreements of onetime friends, or defend against the tactics of a godless society. Like the Israelites in Egypt, we need help.

Thankfully, though we are weak, the God to whom we turn is powerful. The Lord rescued Israel from the clutches of Egypt and overcame their grumbling and mistrust (see Ex. 5:20–23). As today's verses remind us, he was able to do this because he is unlike any other. Singing on the far side of the Red Sea, the Israelites rejoiced in the evidence of God's power. With a flick of his right hand, the earth swallowed his people's enemies. With his strength, he led a congregation

31

prone to infighting toward the place of his holy presence and gave them a song to sing together. With his love, he redeemed sinners to be his own. The Lord is "majestic in holiness, awesome in glorious deeds, doing wonders" (v. 11).

Evidence of God's power is right in front of us too. He has delivered us from our greatest enemy: Satan. By his might, he rescued us from sin's enslavement through Christ's powerful work on the cross. Like the Israelites who amassed evidence of God's past mighty work to give them hope for the future (Ex. 12:17–18), we can take courage from what the Lord has already done for us in Christ.

God can reconcile feuding church members. He can convict sinning elders. He can bring new life to a dying congregation. He can heal wounds. He can give spiritual boldness. Look to God for help. If he is powerful enough to deliver souls from eternal death, he is powerful in whatever situation your church faces today.

Read. Read Exodus 15:1–21. List all the phrases and images that describe God's power. In what ways has God acted powerfully on your behalf in the past? Verses 17–18 of the Israelites' song look ahead to the future. How does reflecting on God's power displayed in the past give you courage for the future?

Reflect. Why does hurt in the church often make us feel vulnerable? What are some situations in your church right now that you are powerless to change? Meditate on the Bible's testimony that our mighty God is able to redeem (Ex. 15:13), reconcile (Eph. 2:14–16), restore (Joel 2:25), and renew (Ezek. 36:26).

Pray. Confess to the Lord that you feel helpless in the face of your church's situation. Tell him about the attacks from outside and the struggles within. Ask him to act in his power.

DAY 14

GOD NEVER CHANGES

*Every good gift and every perfect gift is from above, coming
down from the Father of lights, with whom there is no
variation or shadow due to change. (James 1:17)*

For a time, I was a member of a very large church in an unfamiliar city.
The church was biblically ordered and gospel focused. The generosity
of its many members allowed it to do much good for the cause of
Christ throughout the world. It was a great church. But every Sunday
for weeks, I went home and cried. As someone who had grown up
in a small church, the size of this congregation overwhelmed me.
Each Sunday, I met people, and, each Sunday, they disappeared into
the crowd and I never saw them again. Every week, it felt like I was
walking into a brand-new church.

When church is hard, it can feel like everything is shifting around
us. The churches James was writing to in today's verse were "the
twelve tribes in the Dispersion" (1:1). These first-century congregations had been persecuted, displaced, and scattered. They likely knew
the pain of showing up Sunday to discover empty seats and friends
gone missing. They knew the turmoil of losing pastors and elders and
of sensing hostility toward the church from family and neighbors.
They knew how hard it is to settle into a new church in a new place.

Trouble or changes in the church can cause us to question
whether anything is solid and trustworthy. If pastors and friends come
and go, what can we count on? If the church regularly faces trials of
various kinds (1:2), what can we expect for the future? James points
us to a sure resting place in the midst of unsettling circumstances.
Unlike the shifting shadows we see around us, our God is the same
forever; with him "there is no variation or shadow due to change."

This means God is always at work in his church in both calm and hard times. The same God who "arranged the members in the body, each one of them, as he chose" (1 Cor. 12:18) continues to set people in particular churches. The same God who gave shepherds and teachers to equip the saints (Eph. 4:11–12) continues to provide pastors and elders for us today. The same God who created the church as the testimony of his glory in the world (Eph. 3:9–11) continues to draw sinners to himself through the ministry of local congregations. The same God who appointed the church to send out gospel laborers into spiritually dark places (Matt. 28:18–20) continues to establish new churches where Christ is proclaimed. The same God who appointed Christ as the great shepherd who nurtures, leads, and protects the flock (Heb. 13:20) is the God who promises that "Jesus Christ is the same yesterday and today and forever" (Heb. 13:8).

Why can we trust God when church hurts? Because our God never changes.

Read. Read Psalm 90. What images does the psalmist use to describe God's constancy? What images does he use to illustrate human changeableness? Why is the psalmist able to rejoice at the end of the psalm (vv. 12–17)? How do the truths in this psalm encourage you?

Reflect. Do you have a favorite movie or book that you enjoy over and over, even though you know exactly how the story turns out? Why are familiarity and consistency a comfort? What can you do this week to grow in your knowledge of God so that his constant character will be more familiar to you?

Pray. Praise the Lord because he does not change. Confess to him the ways that you have failed to trust him in your church situation. Ask him to help you rest on him as the one who is "the same yesterday and today and forever" (Heb. 13:8).

DAY 15

GOD IS LOVING

For this reason I bow my knees before the Father . . . [so that you] may have
strength to comprehend with all the saints what is the breadth and length and
height and depth, and to know the love of Christ that surpasses knowledge,
that you may be filled with all the fullness of God. (Eph. 3:14, 18–19)

Church planting in Ephesus was rocky. When Paul first arrived, he
found twelve believers and spent a few months preaching in the
synagogue (Acts 19:1–8). So far, so good. But then slanderers forced
the church to find a new meeting location (v. 9). Later, seven false
prophets co-opted the name of Christ in order to perform exor-
cisms—ending in their spectacular disgrace (vv. 13–16). Then an idol
maker stirred up the whole city to riot against the church (vv. 23–41).

At the end of three years, Paul left Ephesus. He gathered the
church elders and warned them, "After my departure fierce wolves
will come in among you, not sparing the flock; and from among your
own selves will arise men speaking twisted things, to draw away the
disciples after them" (Acts 20:29–30). We can imagine them sighing,
We've faced slanderers, opportunists, and rioters, and now we're going to
have wolves and traitors too?

Today's verses come from Paul's letter to the church at Ephesus,
written sometime after he left. Doubtless, by then they'd endured
additional opposition from within and without. Doubtless, they
were looking for encouragement from their beloved former pastor.
Writing to a beleaguered congregation in a pagan city, Paul says he
wants the church to know God's love. And in our own congregational
troubles, that's what we need to know too.

We see in these verses that God's love for us in Christ has expan-
sive dimensions—it stretches in every direction so far that we need

"strength to comprehend" it. In the same breath that Paul tells them he wants them to comprehend the greatness of God's love, he tells them it actually "surpasses knowledge." God's love is more than our minds can grasp. God's love also has a vast object: "All the saints." The love of God in Christ is poured out on his whole church—all his people, at every time, in every place. Every one of God's acts is always for our good.

When you face wolves and traitors and all kinds of difficulty in the church, you can rest secure. If a congregation member speaks unkindly to you, you can remember that God is always loving. If you are tired of going to church alone, you can take hold of the God who cares for you. If the future of your church looks uncertain, you can call on God to have compassion.

The Lord's love for his church is greater than we can imagine. The One who loved his church so much that he died for her (Eph. 5:25–27) will not abandon us now.

> **Read.** Read Lamentations 3:31–33. When we are hurt, we must remember that, unlike fallen creatures, God never treats us carelessly or unlovingly. All of God's thoughts toward us are always loving all the time, even when he sends trials. How have you experienced God's love in the midst of past afflictions? How do these verses encourage you in your current church struggle?
>
> **Reflect.** Which of the truths we have considered about God's character (sovereignty, power, unchangeableness, love) is particularly precious to you in your current situation? Where do you see that truth expressed in Scripture? How have you experienced it in your life? In what ways can meditating on the other truths also deepen your trust in the Lord?
>
> **Pray.** Ask the Lord to give you "strength to comprehend with all the saints what is the breadth and length and height and depth, and to know the love of Christ that surpasses knowledge" (Eph. 3:18–19).

WHAT CAN I DO?

What happens now? Maybe you've asked yourself this question sitting in the church parking lot after a hard Sunday. I know I have. When the congregational meeting blows up or a dear friend lashes out, it's overwhelming. When you're hurt, it's not easy to choose your next steps.

I wrote this section to help you see what you can do. Whatever your situation, Scripture gives direction for how to respond in a way that honors the Lord. You can start by being sad—expressing your sorrow in words or tears or simply a silent acknowledgement of the grief you feel. You even can do that while you are still in the car after church. Eventually, as you are ready, you can take other steps: pray, get counsel, make a decision about your future in your church.

In these meditations, I'll also caution you against falling into various sins. That might seem like an insensitive thing to do to someone who's hurting, but I'm doing it to alert you to danger. Satan is both a liar and a lion. He doesn't care that you're hurting; in fact, he sees your hurt as his opportunity. He wants to trick you into leaving the safe paths laid out by the Lord, and then he wants to destroy you. It would be unkind for me *not* to warn you about him.

Take a deep breath. Get a drink of water. Open your Bible. And, for today, focus on just one thing you can do now.

DAY 16

EXPRESS SORROW

*And at the evening sacrifice I rose from my fasting, with my
garment and my cloak torn, and fell upon my knees and spread
out my hands to the LORD my God, saying: "O my God, I am
ashamed and blush to lift my face to you, my God, for our
iniquities have risen higher than our heads." (Ezra 9:5–6)*

After a four-month journey, Ezra and the exiles arrived in Jerusalem
(Ezra 7:8–9). At long last, they sacrificed to God in the place of his
presence with the exiles who had returned before (8:35). What a
joy finally to be reunited with God's people in worship! But their
excitement was short-lived. As soon as the worship service was over,
the leaders already living in Jerusalem approached Ezra with heart-
wrenching news. The earlier group of exiles may have settled back
in the land, but they had failed to obey God. Rather than separating
from their pagan neighbors, the Israelites—including the priests
and Levites—had married idol worshippers (9:1–2). Having risked
everything to escape the idolatry of Babylon, Ezra found the same
sins rampant in the congregation of God's people.

What Ezra did next shows us how we can respond when sin
comes to light in our own congregations. Ezra immediately ("as soon
as I heard this," v. 3) began to mourn. He tore his garments and pulled
out his hair, adopting the culturally recognized markers of deep grief.
Other faithful members of the congregation—"all who trembled at
the words of the God of Israel" (v. 4)—mourned alongside him. For
hours, he "sat appalled" (vv. 3, 4), overwhelmed by the wickedness
among people who were meant to be holy.

In the evening, Ezra took his grief to the Lord. He fell on his
knees, spread out his hands, and prayed with "weeping and casting

himself down before the house of God" (10:1). He confessed the sin of God's people, unflinchingly describing their "evil deeds and . . . great guilt" (9:13) and acknowledging the Lord's perfect right to be angry with them (v. 14). As he prayed, many others joined him, and they all wept together (10:1).

When we, like Ezra, encounter sin and hurt in the church, it's right that we grieve. If a pastor's scandalous sin is exposed, if church members incite disunity, if the weak in the church are neglected, if professing believers depart from Christ—we should sit appalled as soon as we hear of it. In the same way that we would immediately mourn the death of a loved one, we ought to mourn the loss of righteousness among God's people. And as we mourn, we should pray, expressing our sorrow to the God who hears and cares, the God of justice and the God of mercy.

Read. Read Ezra 9:6–15. What words and phrases does Ezra use for sin? How does his language affirm the horror of lawlessness? Why does the Lord's kindness to his people in redeeming them from exile (vv. 8–9) make it all the more appalling that they would then disobey him (vv. 13–14)? How have we been redeemed by the Lord? Why is it therefore particularly grievous when Christians sin?

Reflect. Is sorrow your first response when you hear of sin or experience the effects of sin in your church body? Why or why not? The next time you find out about some unrighteousness in your congregation, take time as soon as possible to be appalled, to mourn, and to pray.

Pray. Come before the Lord with the words of Ezra: "O my God, I am ashamed and blush to lift my face to you, my God, for our iniquities have risen higher than our heads" (v. 6).

DAY 17

BEWARE BITTERNESS

Be angry and do not sin; do not let the sun go down on your
anger, and give no opportunity to the devil. . . . Let all bitterness
and wrath and anger and clamor and slander be put away
from you, along with all malice. (Eph. 4:26–27, 31)

My mother-in-law has Parkinson's disease. She takes multiple daily medications, keeps up with current medical research, and schedules appointments with specialists who oversee parts of her care. Managing this illness requires huge amounts of her attention. But Parkinson's isn't the only threat to her health. "I have to force myself to schedule my annual mammogram," she once told me. "I'd like to think Parkinson's is my one bad thing to get, but that's not necessarily true. I could have cancer too."

When church hurts, it can be easy to think the hard situation is our "one bad thing to get" and relax our vigilance against other threats. The lingering church conflict, wandering church member, or abdicating church leader consumes all our attention, and we forget that sin is crouching at other doors too. Like a lion, Satan would like nothing better than to pounce on the wounded and unguarded members of the flock to bring them down when they least expect it (1 Peter 5:8). Today's verses warn us that the devil is looking for an opening, and he'll gladly exploit trouble in our churches in order to incite sin in our hearts. Knowing this, we must beware.

In hard church circumstances, we may be angry, but we cannot allow our anger to become sinful and bitter. Paul warns us that such anger is an opportunity for the devil to lead us into further sin and, ultimately, to destruction. Instead, we must submit our hearts to the Lord and ask for his help. The devil would like us to throw off all restraint; the Lord calls us to resist bitterness and imitate him (v. 32), navigating the precarious line between "be angry" and "do not sin."

Each hurt and doubt and conflict in the church is part of Satan's relentless war against the children of God (Rev. 12:17). When we surrender to bitterness, we allow the devil a double triumph: not only has he sown trouble in the congregation, he's also used that turmoil to provoke sin in our hearts. But thanks be to God, Satan does not have the last word over us. Through the power of Christ's blood and the help of the Holy Spirit, we can "resist the devil, and he will flee" (James 4:7).

> **Read.** Read Genesis 4:1–16. How did Cain respond to the Lord's correction of his improper worship? What did the Lord warn him was happening (v. 7)? What was the result when Cain failed to heed the Lord's warning? Where is sin "crouching at the door" in your own responses to situations in the church?

> **Reflect.** Puritan Thomas Brooks wrote, "Sin gives Satan a power over us, and an advantage to accuse us and to lay claim to us, as those that wear his badge." In the midst of church hurt, remember that Satan doesn't care that you are weak and suffering. In fact, he sees it as his opportunity. He wants you to sin so he can have a reason to accuse you and power to tempt you further. Beware!

> **Pray.** Tell the Lord about the ways you are being tempted to bitterness in your current situation. Confess the times you have already fallen into sin. Ask him to forgive you, to keep you from temptation, and to enable you to stand firm when you are tempted (Matt. 6:12–13). Praise him for triumphing over sin and Satan (Col. 2:15).

DAY 18

CONFESS SIN

Let your ear be attentive and your eyes open, to hear the prayer of your
servant that I now pray before you day and night for the people of Israel
your servants, confessing the sins of the people of Israel, which we have
sinned against you. Even I and my father's house have sinned. (Neh. 1:6)

Nehemiah was eager to hear how God's people in Jerusalem were
doing. As soon as his brother Hanani arrived at his house, Nehemiah
asked him for a full report about the congregation. Sadly, the news
was not good. The people, Hanani said, were "in great trouble and
shame" (Neh. 1:3). Their gathering place was in ruins (2:3) and they
were the constant butt of their neighbors' scorn (v. 17). Seemingly
nothing was going well for them.

When our own congregations seem to be in ruins—when spiritual
zeal ebbs, when members depart, when our unbelieving neighbors
think the church is a joke or a threat—we can look to Nehemiah to
learn what to do. And his response may surprise us. Today's verse
tells us that when Nehemiah heard that God's people were shamed
and brought low, his first act was to confess sin. He confessed the sin
of the congregation, and he confessed his own sin: "Even I and my
father's house have sinned." Although Nehemiah was living far from
Jerusalem, he didn't assume anyone was blameless. Whenever the
church is in trouble, we should examine our hearts and see if there is
any transgression we ought to confess to the Lord.

Not every hardship is a result of specific sin, of course. Jesus
reminded us that sometimes trials come on people simply so God's
mysterious purposes may be accomplished (John 9:1–3). But other
times, our sins do have direct consequences in the church. The Lord
warned the congregation at Thyatira that they would face trouble

if they continued to tolerate sin, and members of the Corinthian church even died because of their failure to worship rightly (Rev. 2:20–23; 1 Cor. 11:29–31). Although we may not know in every instance whether a particular sin has brought God's fatherly chastisement (Heb. 12:5–11) on our congregation, we do know that we each sin daily and continually stand in need of Christ's cleansing blood. When the church is in trouble, confessing our own sin brings us into a posture of humble dependence on God and allows us to take further action with a clear conscience before the Lord.

Ultimately, our confession is a hopeful act. Nehemiah asked God to have an attentive ear and an open eye, confident that Yahweh was ready to forgive those who confess. We too can come boldly to the throne of grace, knowing our Lord has promised that "if we confess our sins, he is faithful and just to forgive us our sins and to cleanse us from all unrighteousness" (1 John 1:9).

> **Read.** Read Ezra 10:1–11. What was the sin of the congregation? How did they respond? What can we learn from the fact that the women and children assembled too? Why were the people trembling (v. 9)? What does this tell us about their attitude toward their sin?
>
> **Reflect.** Romans 3 reminds us "none is righteous, no, not one" (v. 10) and "all have sinned and fall short of the glory of God" (v. 23). When trouble comes on our church, why is it important to acknowledge our own sin?
>
> **Pray.** Cry out to the Lord, telling him that your church "is in great trouble and shame" (Neh. 1:3). Confess, "We have sinned against you" and "even I . . . have sinned" (v. 6). Ask him to "grant . . . mercy" (v. 11).

DAY 19

BEWARE SELF-RIGHTEOUSNESS

Two men went up into the temple to pray, one a Pharisee and the other a tax collector. The Pharisee, standing by himself, prayed thus: "God, I thank you that I am not like other men, extortioners, unjust, adulterers, or even like this tax collector. I fast twice a week; I give tithes of all that I get." But the tax collector, standing far off, would not even lift up his eyes to heaven, but beat his breast, saying, "God, be merciful to me, a sinner!" I tell you, this man went down to his house justified, rather than the other. For everyone who exalts himself will be humbled, but the one who humbles himself will be exalted. (Luke 18:10–14)

In his classic book, *Precious Remedies against Satan's Devices*, Thomas Brooks lists several "devices" Satan uses to draw us to sin. "Satan," he explains, "being fallen from light to darkness, from felicity to misery, from heaven to hell, from an angel to a devil, is so full of malice and envy that he will leave no means unattempted, whereby he may make all others eternally miserable with himself." One of his chief tools to create misery is causing Christians to "be frequent in comparing themselves or their ways with those that are reputed or reported to be worse than themselves." Satan likes nothing better than to encourage you to be self-righteous.

Especially when we are feeling hurt in the church, the Evil One has plenty of these opportunities. It's all too easy for him to nudge us to create a mental score sheet of the ways people have hurt us or to be consumed with the obvious wrongdoings of others—and to judge ourselves not so bad by comparison. This was the devilish device that felled the Pharisee in today's verses. When he came to worship, his eyes darted around to others with a public record of sin. The tax collector, in particular, became the object of the Pharisee's scorn and the grounds for his pride.

The Pharisee wasn't wrong about the tax collector. This was a man who had taken advantage of and hurt others, and he may have even stolen from the Pharisee. (After all, the Pharisee immediately recognized him!) The Pharisee wasn't wrong about the tax collector, but he was wrong about himself. As he looked around rather than looking to the Lord, the Pharisee measured himself against the actions of others and failed to see his own sin. By convincing the Pharisee he didn't need forgiveness, Satan neatly cut him off from the Lord's tender mercy. The tax collector, and not the Pharisee, went home justified—washed in the blood of the Son, reconciled to the Father, and securely held by the Spirit.

When we feel hurt, it can be tempting to become self-righteous. Muddled by Satan, we don't see our need of a Savior, and we justify ourselves by looking at others' wicked actions. But Christ offers us a better vision, warning us against falling prey to Satan's devices and showing us that the joy of true justification comes only by way of humility.

> **Read.** Read Matthew 7:1–5. What does Jesus mean by a "speck" and a "log"? Why are we often more attentive to others' specks than our own logs? How does church hurt exacerbate this?
>
> **Reflect.** Thomas Brooks warns that Satan would have us be "quick-sighted abroad and blind at home." In what ways are you poised to see the sins of others? Where might you be blind to your own? How does this device aid Satan's aim for your soul?
>
> **Pray.** Pray the tax collector's words: "God, be merciful to me, a sinner!"

DAY 20

TRUST THE LORD

If it had not been the LORD who was on our side—let Israel now say—
if it had not been the LORD who was on our side when people rose up
against us, then they would have swallowed us up alive. (Ps. 124:1–3)

Every Sunday, on the ride to church, our family sings. One of us suggests a familiar hymn or psalm, and we use it to tune our voices and souls in preparation for worship. Some days, my heart is light and eager to gather with the church; praises burst from my lips with joy. Other times, I'm weighed down by trouble; singing on the way to church feels like a deliberate choice. On those Sundays, I have to discipline my mouth and heart to affirm what God says about himself: he is sovereign, he is good, he is trustworthy.

The Psalms of Ascent (120–134) are a songbook for going to worship. These are the psalms Israelites sang as they journeyed to Jerusalem for the prescribed feasts and sacrifices. Today's verses come from Psalm 124 and acknowledge that God's people sometimes go up to worship with a heavy heart. In David's psalm, the traveling worshippers were a bedraggled bunch. They faced an onslaught of anger from their enemies. To the faithful men and women on the road to Jerusalem, it felt like a raging flood (vv. 4–5), the teeth of a wild beast (v. 6), and the snare of a hunter (v. 7) all at once. It seemed like attacks were coming from every side.

But just when the flood was going over their heads, the jaws were snapping shut, and the trap was about to spring, help arrived! "The LORD, who made heaven and earth" (v. 8) came to his people's aid. With these words, the singers affirm that God is sovereign. He is the Creator of all things and therefore all things are under his command. Twice they marvel at what would have happened "if it had not been the LORD who was on our side" (vv. 1, 2), declaring that God is unfailingly good. The Lord who had made a covenant with them and their fathers before them was the one who came alongside them to rescue them from trouble. And so, as they walked the difficult road to the place of worship, they sang.

When church hurts and we ask ourselves, *What can I do?* Psalm 124 provides an answer. Like God's people of old, we can trust the Lord. We can call to mind who he is (as we saw on days 12–15) and then place our confidence in him, believing that he will do what is right. In this world—and even on the way to worship—we may face opposition, but we need not fear because the Lord is on our side.

Read. Read Psalm 121, a song of ascents. What are the singers of this psalm looking for (v. 1)? List the truths about God in this psalm that comforted the worshippers on their way to Jerusalem. How can those truths encourage you as you go to worship?

Reflect. How do you spend the time on your way to church on Sunday? Consider whether you could sing, read Scripture, or pray during those moments. Write down a song or passage of Scripture for next Sunday that would remind you of God's sovereignty and goodness and that would encourage you to trust God even when going to church is hard.

Pray. Use the language of Psalm 124. Tell the Lord about your church situation: the enemies of God who oppose you, the anger you face from others, the flood of trouble that threatens to overwhelm you, and the temptations to sin that wait for you like baited traps. Praise him as your Creator and Helper. Ask him to help you trust that he is on your side to deliver you from evil.

DAY 21

BEWARE DOUBT

Count it all joy, my brothers and sisters, when you meet trials of various kinds, for you know that the testing of your faith produces steadfastness. . . . If any of you lacks wisdom, let him ask God, who gives generously to all without reproach, and it will be given him. But let him ask in faith, with no doubting, for the one who doubts is like a wave of the sea that is driven and tossed by the wind. For that person must not suppose that he will receive anything from the Lord; he is a double-minded man, unstable in all his ways. (James 1:2–3, 5–8)

The first believers who experienced doubt came from a small congregation. Things were actually going along just fine: the congregation members worked hard, had fellowship with each other, and worshipped God together. But Satan had other plans. Approaching one of the members, he asked her the question that lives in infamy: "Did God actually say, 'You shall not eat of any tree in the garden'?" (Gen. 3:1). By his query, and his crafty follow-ups, Satan planted seeds of doubt in the woman's mind and heart. *Does God speak truth? Does God do what's best? Is God good?* The woman's doubt made her waver, and she gave in to sin—with disastrous effects.

If Satan saw an opportunity to sow doubt in Eve—whose congregation of worshippers had everything good and beautiful it could ever need (Gen. 2:8–10)—how much more will he see a chance in us when our hearts and churches are struggling?

You may be wondering, *How could the Lord allow me to keep going to church year after year without my spouse and children? How could God allow me to be sinned against by my elders? How could the Lord allow our congregation to see so little fruit?* In the midst of your hurt, Satan is ready to incite doubt: *Is God actually trustworthy?*

49

James knows this, and in today's verses he tells us three things.

First, he explains why the Lord allows us to experience hardship. Our "various trials" are intended by a good God to increase our faith and make us steadfast. When we are weakened by suffering, we can be strong, because we have arrived at a place where we have no option except to cast ourselves on the Lord's strength (2 Cor. 12:7–10).

Second, James tells us what to do in trials. We should "ask God . . . in faith" for the wisdom to navigate them well. If our trials are to produce spiritual fruit in us, we need the help of our sovereign and good God.

Third, James tells us what to beware of: doubt. When we doubt God, we become "double-minded" and "unstable," an easy target for Satan's schemes and the world's lies. Instead, we must come to God in faith—believing that he is who he says he is and that he cares for those who trust him (Heb. 11:6).

Read. Read Hebrews 11. List some of the difficulties God's people navigated by faith. How does their example encourage you to beware of doubt and to cling to the Lord? How might God use your steadfastness in your current trials to encourage others?

Reflect. It's become popular to assert that doubt is an inevitable—even admirable—part of faith. The testimony of Scripture, however, is that while doubts may plague believers, doubts are never to be indulged. What do today's verses show you about the nature of doubt?

Pray. Tell the Lord about a situation where Satan is provoking doubt in your heart. Using the words of today's verses, ask him to give you wisdom and steadfast faith in him.

DAY 22

SEEK HELP FROM GOD

I waited patiently for the LORD; he inclined to me and heard my cry. (Ps. 40:1)

Several years ago, our church was struggling. We owned a building that was poorly located and poorly laid out for the needs of our congregation. For years, we tried to sell the building, but, unfortunately, it wasn't an ideal facility for anyone else either. Again and again a potential buyer would arise, only to fall through. Meanwhile, the land we had purchased in another town lay bare. Our congregation was small, spent, and stuck.

Recalling the example of Queen Esther, who gathered God's people in prayer when their future looked bleak (Est. 4:16), our elders called a church-wide fast to seek the Lord. In our prayer meeting, we begged God to give us wisdom, show us mercy, and bring us into a place of fruitful ministry. The Lord didn't immediately answer our prayers for a new building, but he did strengthen our hearts as we looked to him. When the church seems like it's on the brink of collapse—whether from trouble without or within—we must seek help from the Lord.

In Psalm 40, where we find today's verse, David too was beset by "evils . . . beyond number" (v. 12). He was overwhelmed by his own sin: "my iniquities have overtaken me" (v. 12). He had also been sinned against by others: "[those] who seek to snatch away my life . . . who delight in my hurt!" (v. 14). The "miry bog" (v. 2) that sucked at David's life was—like many messy situations in our own lives—partly of his own making and partly others' fault. And, like Esther, David knew his only hope was in crying out to God (v. 1).

David knew and trusted God ("you are my help and my deliverer," v. 17) and so he sought the Lord's help in his troubles. He asked the Lord to rescue him both from his own sin and from the devices of others. Although he asked the Lord to "make haste" (v. 13), he knew God's answer might not be immediate. He "waited patiently," trusting that the Lord would hear and act at just the right time. In our own hardship in the church, we can learn from David's persistent cry to God for help. If we are caught in sin or being sinned against, if we are perilously close to a "pit of destruction" (v. 2), we should ask the Lord for wisdom (v. 4), sanctification (v. 8), forgiveness (v. 11), deliverance (v. 13), justice (v. 14), and comfort (v. 17). Perhaps surprisingly, we can also ask him for joy (v. 16).

Psalm 40 shows us that crying out to God is not only good for us, it's also good for the other members of our congregation, giving us an opportunity to testify of God's goodness before them. When the Lord didn't restrain his mercy from David (v. 11), David didn't restrain his lips from praising the Lord (v. 9). In this way, our difficulties in the church can become a blessing to the church as we call on "the great congregation" to behold with us the steadfast love and faithfulness of our God (v. 10).

Read. Read Psalm 40. What truths about God's character does David affirm? What other truths about God could you add from other parts of Scripture? How does knowing these things encourage you to cry out to him?

Reflect. Esther and the people of God sought the Lord with prayer and fasting. They refrained from eating and drinking in order to wean themselves from the temporary comforts of this world, to remind themselves of their dependence on God, and to orient their hearts and schedules toward seeking his mercy. Consider fasting about your own hard church situation, either on your own or with a group of church members.

Pray. Using the words of Psalm 40, tell the Lord about the "miry bog" that has you trapped today (v. 2). Confess your own sins (v. 12). Lament the times you have been sinned against (vv. 14–15). Cry to the Lord: "Make haste to help me!" (v. 13). Commit to one day telling others about the ways he delivered you (v. 9).

DAY 23

BEWARE PRIDE

Blessed is the man who makes the LORD his trust, who does not turn to the proud, to those who go astray after a lie! (Ps. 40:4)

"How could the elders do that?" I asked my husband through tears after a congregational meeting. I was hurt that they had made the choice to discipline a friend whom I saw as more wronged than wrong. "Don't they know the whole story?" I proceeded to tell my husband, our church's pastor, how I perceived the situation and what I thought the elders had missed.

"Yes," my husband said, "they know those things. But they also know some things you don't." In my hurt, I was blind to my ignorance and foolishly convinced myself that I knew what was best.

In yesterday's meditation, we saw the importance of seeking help from God in times of trouble. Today, we turn again to Psalm 40 and see that David acknowledges the danger of relying on ourselves—the danger of pride—when we are struggling.

When we are feeling hurt in church, Satan is ready to cut us off from the source of true help—the Lord—and deceive us into trusting ourselves and our own judgments. The situation in our congregation may seem abundantly clear to us. We may think we know who is right and who is wrong, we may think we know exactly what needs to be done next, and we can assume we are the perfect people to do it. But Psalm 40 urges us to avoid the devil's trap. The one who doesn't indulge his pride but who "makes the Lord his trust" is blessed.

Especially when we have been sinned against, we often want justice immediately and can take matters into our own hands, no matter what we might need to compromise. Pride encourages us to pursue speedy results for ourselves in any way possible, but David received true deliverance when he "waited patiently for the LORD" (v. 1). Being hurt can also cause us to feel vulnerable, and so we may be tempted to rely on "the proud"—on those who have obvious power and ability in this world—even if they lead us astray. Following ungodly advice from ungodly people may seem empowering, but Scripture tells us it's the path of misery (Prov. 14:12; 16:25).

As David knew, blessing comes from seeking the Lord and delight comes from following his Word (Ps. 40:8). We can come to him in prayer, admitting our weakness and asking him for his wisdom. We can confess the ways we've thought much of ourselves and our own plans. We can read his Word and submit ourselves to his revealed will. We can look for godly men and women (as we'll see in the next meditation) and ask for their wise counsel. We can ask for his help to resist Satan's temptations to "go astray after a lie." When church hurts, we can't afford to trust in ourselves.

> **Read.** Read Isaiah 31:1–5. What is the problem with relying on ourselves and on those who seem to have power in this world? Where is our true help found?
>
> **Reflect.** Romans 12:16 warns us, "Never be wise in your own sight." Why is pride dangerous? Why is it tempting? Write this verse out and put it somewhere where you can often see it.
>
> **Pray.** Confess the ways you have fallen into the trap of pride in your current situation—thinking you know exactly what is happening and what should be done. Ask the Lord to forgive you and to help you trust him rather than yourself.

DAY 24

SEEK HELP FROM
WISE COUNSELORS

Where there is no guidance, a people falls, but in an
abundance of counselors there is safety. (Prov. 11:14)

When God's people left Egypt, they brought their livestock and
their sin with them. They had conflicts over property, conflicts over
relationships, conflicts over inheritances, conflicts over contracts,
conflicts over petty crimes, conflicts over major injustices. There
were so many disputes in the assembly that Moses had to hear cases
all day every day (Ex. 18:13–16). In fact, after dispensing all that
counsel, Moses needed counsel himself (vv. 17–23)! A congregation
of two million members produces a lot of strife.

To help his people, the Lord provided wise counselors—"men
who fear God, who are trustworthy and hate a bribe"—to solve
disputes and to enable the congregation members to "go to their
place in peace" (vv. 21, 23).

Just like the people of Israel, God's people today need counsel in
the midst of conflicts and hurt. As today's verse shows us, we often
make poor decisions on our own. Swayed by our own desires and
our limited perspective and wisdom, we often choose the wrong
course of action, which can lead to harm. Instead, we need the help
of others to know how to proceed.

When we are hurt in the church, usually our best counselors will
be the elders of the church. Those are the men God has appointed
and who display the wisdom and grace needed to shepherd God's
people in the church (Titus 1:5–9). Your pastors and elders are tasked

by God with keeping watch over your soul (Heb. 13:17); don't be reluctant to ask them for help.

But if the elders of your own church are part of the problem, seek counsel from other mature believers or elders in another church. In the early church, when the dispute over circumcision couldn't be solved locally, Paul and Barnabas called on apostles and elders from throughout the region to help them (Acts 15:1–35). Sometimes we too may have to get help from outside our congregation.

Ultimately, we should look for counselors who display godly (not worldly) wisdom. Scripture tells us this wisdom is "first pure, then peaceable, gentle, open to reason, full of mercy and good fruits, impartial and sincere" (James 3:17). When church hurts, this kind of counsel from mature believers is one of God's tools to shepherd our hearts away from danger and toward healing.

Read. Read Numbers 27:1–11. What was the problem the daughters of Zelophehad had? To whom did they go for help? What was the result? How did the women serve God's people in the future by bringing their case to the elders? How might your own situation—and the future of your church—be helped by your getting wise counsel?

Reflect. It's vital to choose wise and godly people as counselors. Although it might feel satisfying to seek advice from someone who immediately takes our side, Moses looked for "men who fear God, who are trustworthy and hate a bribe" (Ex. 18:21). Think of two or three people you know who love the Lord, know his Word, seek him by prayer, live Christlike lives, avoid partiality, and are respected by other believers. Consider asking them to help you think through your situation.

Pray. Ask the Lord to give you "an abundance of counselors" who can help you wisely navigate your circumstances.

DAY 25

BEWARE ISOLATION

Whoever isolates himself seeks his own desire; he breaks
out against all sound judgment. (Prov. 18:1)

After years of obeying the Lord at great cost to himself while God's
people fell into apostasy around him, Elijah couldn't take it anymore.
He left the people and headed for the wilderness—alone. There,
he retreated into a cave. When the Lord spoke to him, asking him
twice why a prophet would stay away from the congregation he
was sent to serve, twice Elijah had a ready answer: "The people of
Israel have forsaken your covenant, thrown down your altars, and
killed your prophets with the sword, and I, even I only, am left, and
they seek my life, to take it away" (1 Kings 19:10, 14). *I feel alone, so
I've decided to be alone.*

In response, the Lord graciously drew near to Elijah (vv. 11–13).
With a display of his power and his mercy, he reminded Elijah that
he was not, in fact, alone. But then the Lord did something we might
not expect. He sent Elijah to rejoin the congregation (vv. 15–21).
The Lord revealed his plan to resolve Israel's problem—by bringing
justice against the wicked and showing mercy to the righteous—and
he gave Elijah directions to find another faithful man, Elisha, to assist
him. When Elijah wanted to isolate himself, God sent him back to
the assembly to get help.

When we are hurt, it can be uncomfortable to be in the congregation and to seek the help of others. Sometimes we are ashamed;
sometimes the problems are so painful it feels impossible to talk
about them; sometimes we'd rather try to deal with the situation in
our own way; sometimes, like Elijah, we've been hurt by people so
we don't trust that people may be part of the solution. The Bible,

however, warns us against becoming isolated, even when (especially when!) we are struggling. In yesterday's verse, Solomon urged us to get godly counsel for our own safety. In today's verse, he highlights the danger of cutting ourselves off from other believers.

Throughout Scripture, we see that an isolated Christian is a Christian in peril. Comparing scattered believers to sheep, the prophet Ezekiel laments how they "became food for all the wild beasts" (Ezek. 34:5). And Jesus explains how believers without pastoral care are vulnerable to the wolf who "snatches them and scatters them" (John 10:12). A lone sheep wandering on a cliff edge is not safe; that's just where an opportunistic wolf would like him to be.

Dear Christian, don't be naive. The Evil One—that "roaring lion" (1 Peter 5:8)—would like to keep you isolated. As he draws you away from the preaching of the Word, the prayers of God's people, and the opportunity for godly counsel, he also whispers lies into your soul (John 8:44) convincing you that God doesn't care, that other Christians aren't good for you, and that what *you* desire in this moment must be right. Don't let him get you alone.

Read. Read Isaiah 40:9–11. What do these verses say the Lord does for his sheep? Why is being part of a flock good for sheep? Do you think of being part of the church as "good news" (v. 9)? How do these verses shape your thinking?

Reflect. Why does Satan love to isolate us? What sins are we especially vulnerable to when we are alone?

Pray. Confess to the Lord that you often feel alone in your church situation. Ask him to keep you from isolating yourself. Plead with him to show you the goodness of being among his people and getting help there.

DAY 26

DECIDE TO STAY—OR GO

Now Barnabas wanted to take with them John called Mark.
But Paul thought best not to take with them one who had
withdrawn from them in Pamphylia and had not gone with
them to the work. And there arose a sharp disagreement, so
that they separated from each other. (Acts 15:37–39)

Paul and Barnabas were a gospel team. They had labored side-by-side to bring the gospel of Christ to various cities along the Mediterranean (Acts 13–14). Together they worked miracles, planted churches, and survived violent persecution. They even organized a church council to address false teaching (15:1–35). Time after time, they made the choice to cooperate in kingdom work, but today's verses expose a breach in their unity.

While Paul thought John Mark couldn't be trusted to accompany them on their next trip, Barnabas thought he should come along. In the end, Paul went one way and Barnabas another.

They didn't part ways lightly. More than simply a dispute over John Mark, this conflict was about qualification for ministry, the process for restoring trust, and the good of the church. At times, people doing ministry together reach an impasse over the best way to work for the glory of God and the benefit of his kingdom.

This narrative (and its conclusion, which we will see in the next meditation) highlights God's power to advance the gospel and establish his church despite trouble, but it also acknowledges that Christians sometimes disagree and even break fellowship for a time.

The difficulties in your own church may mean you'll need to consider whether or not to remain in that congregation. When we consider whether to leave a church, we first need to ask ourselves whether the issues at hand are truly significant. In Scripture (and in Paul's own writings!), divisions based on preference are a sign of immaturity (1 Cor. 3:1–9), petty quarrels are contrary to the gospel of Christ (2 Tim. 2:23), and it's our "glory" to overlook an offense (Prov. 19:11). Minor disagreements aren't worth separating over. What's more, in any issue, our first step is always to pursue resolution in the hope of being able to stay (1 Peter 4:8; Matt. 5:23–24; 18:15–20). But irreconcilable issues that strike at gospel essentials or cause us to go against our biblically informed conscience, or situations where the church fails to address known sin, may mean we need to go.

The biblical truths from the previous meditations in this book will help in this decision. It requires great wisdom to determine if you should stay or go. You'll need to seek the Spirit's help in prayer, study the wisdom of God revealed in Scripture, and receive counsel from mature believers. Ultimately, you'll need to make a decision and move forward, trusting God with the results, and—as we will see in the next meditation—seeking to honor the Lord in whatever you choose to do.

Read. Read Proverbs 3:1–12. What does Solomon say are the benefits of walking in wisdom? What does he give as the source of true wisdom? What do these verses teach you about your greatest need as you decide about your hard church situation?

Reflect. "I made up my mind not to make another painful visit to you" wrote Paul to the Corinthian church (2 Cor. 2:1). Why is it important to eventually make up your mind when considering whether to stay or go in a particular church situation? What are some harmful effects of always waffling and never deciding?

Pray. Cry out to the Lord for wisdom about whether you should stay or go. Ask him to be faithful to his promise to give wisdom to those who ask (James 1:5).

DAY 27

BEWARE STRIFE

Barnabas took Mark with him and sailed away to Cyprus, but
Paul chose Silas and departed, having been commended by the
brothers to the grace of the Lord. And he went through Syria
and Cilicia, strengthening the churches. (Acts 15:39–41)

Paul and Barnabas's story doesn't end with their choice to part ways.
Even after they made up their minds about leaving, they still had to
decide how to relate to the rest of the church, to other churches, and
to each other. Paul sought to do this wisely, and the elders of the
church at Antioch "commended [him] . . . to the grace of the Lord"
(v. 40). Even in their separation, Paul and Barnabas still had to resist
Satan's schemes and pursue God's honor.

Whether you decide to stay in or leave your church, beware the
temptation to contribute to discord among believers. If you leave,
you will need to leave honorably—being truthful with the elders
about your reasons for leaving, following the process your church
has for removing your membership, and humbly remaining open to
reconciliation and resolution. If you choose to stay, you will need to
trust God with that decision and continue to uphold the vows you
took when you joined the church.

After leaving Antioch, Paul took up the good of Christ's body
in other places, "strengthening the churches." He and Barnabas may
have chosen to break fellowship, but neither of them was finished
with the church. Instead, both of them continued to serve the
body for the rest of their lives. If you choose to leave your church,
you will need to move on well—joining another biblical church as
soon as possible and using your gifts for the good of God's people
there. If you stay, you will need to trust that God has work for you

61

to do and not allow Satan to tempt you to withhold good from your congregation.

Acts 15 is not the last we hear from Paul about John Mark. In later letters, Paul instructs the church to welcome Mark (Col. 4:10), commends Mark for his kingdom usefulness (2 Tim. 4:11), and calls him his fellow worker (Philem. 1:24). Although Mark was the reason for Paul's departure, he wasn't the object of Paul's disdain. If you leave your church, you will still need to do good to the congregation you've left. You should continue to pray for them, rejoice with them when they grow in holiness and bear fruit, and speak well of them however you truthfully can. If you stay, you should pursue kindness and not allow the Evil One to provoke you to gossip or slander, setting congregation members against one another. Like Abram interceding for Lot (Gen. 18:22–33), whether you stay or go you should seek the good of believers with whom you disagree.

> **Read.** Read Genesis 13:2–13; 14:14–16; 18:22–33. Why did Lot and Abram part ways? Where did Lot move? After their separation, Abram continued to help Lot and seek his good. What did Abram do? What do these passages teach us about righteous conduct toward others—even others we've had to separate from?
>
> **Reflect.** Solomon wrote, "It is an honor for a man to keep aloof from strife, but every fool will be quarreling" (Prov. 20:3). Which is harder: avoiding strife or joining quarrels? Why? Where do you feel that tension in your church situation?
>
> **Pray.** Tell the Lord about the times you have been tempted to stir up strife with gossip, unkindness, or lies. Ask him to keep you from the Evil One and help you do good to your church instead. Thank him for being the God who never withholds good from his people (Ps. 84:11).

WHY SHOULD I KEEP SHOWING UP?

When the alarm beeps on Sunday morning, you might feel like shutting it off and rolling over. Your neighbors aren't rushing out the door to confront their disappointments and sorrows this morning. They're sleeping or gardening or drinking coffee on the front porch or heading to the beach. Over the past weeks—even years—church has become a hard place for you, and it's not always obvious why you should keep making the effort to show up.

In the next six meditations, we're going to see that Scripture gives us precious reasons to commit to the church, even when it's hard. The reasons I've chosen are deeper and more valuable than many of the motivations we often have for church participation; they're better than unquestionably good things like friendship, support, wise counsel, and opportunities to serve. They're better because they aren't about other people, or even about us. They're better because they're about Jesus.

As you read, maybe just one of these six reasons will stick with you. That's okay. Take that reason. Write it on a notecard. Put it where you'll see it when the alarm goes off. Let it get you out of bed and into church one more time. I promise: Jesus is worth it.

CHRIST ESTABLISHED HIS CHURCH

And [the Father] put all things under [Christ's] feet and gave
him as head over all things to the church, which is his body,
the fullness of him who fills all in all. (Eph. 1:22–23)

Years ago, I joined our neighborhood association board. The elected members met once a month to attempt to keep the neighborhood safe and beautiful and to adjudicate issues. We authorized maintenance, filed permits, balanced budgets, and received angry letters from our neighbors. I came to dread the hours-long meetings, and, after a while, I resigned and never looked back.

Neighborhood associations do some good in the world, but they aren't mandatory, and their members are perfectly free to quit at any time. Likewise, any number of other institutions and associations in this world have limited claims on our time and energy. In the PTA or at the gym, we join at our choosing and participate at our discretion.

The church, however, is no mere human institution. As we begin to answer the question "Why should I keep showing up?" we see that the unique character of the church is what compels our continued commitment to it, even when it's hard. Today's verses teach us that the church was established by God and given to Christ. In a passage of effusive thanksgiving savoring the goodness of God's creating and electing and redeeming work, the pinnacle of Paul's reason for praise is the lordship of Christ over his church. The church is under Christ's feet; he is over the church as its head.

As head of the church, Christ pours out his Spirit and indwells his church, filling it with his fullness. We see this most clearly in the church's weekly gathering for worship. Christ speaks to us in the preaching of the Word (1 Thess. 2:13). He prays with us in the corporate prayers of his gathered people (Rom. 8:34). He calls us to sing together and draws our hearts to praise (Heb. 2:12). He gives us confidence to confess our faith (Heb. 4:14–16). He seals us for his own in the visible, tangible signs of baptism and the Lord's Supper (Rom. 6:4; 1 Cor. 11:24). Sunday after Sunday, Christ comes to his church, ministers his grace, and displays his glory.

When we are hurt, we might be tempted to give up and walk away from the church, but the Scripture tells us that would be to our detriment. Even if we choose to stop showing up, Jesus never will. The church is the place of Christ's visible reign and is where he ordains the means of grace we desperately need. Although church membership is often neither convenient nor comfortable, we can be encouraged that Christ established his church and we can trust that he has good for us in it.

Read. Read Ephesians 4:8–16. Who was the one who ascended? What gifts did he give? What is the purpose of those gifts? How does the truth that Christ rules and equips his church help you to see the church as a unique institution?

Reflect. What are some human organizations you have joined in the past? In what ways is commitment to the church different from commitment to those organizations?

Pray. Confess to the Lord the ways you find it hard to continue showing up in your local church. Ask him for help to trust his good purposes in establishing the church. Plead with him to show you his fullness as you commit to being part of his body.

DAY 29

CHRIST LOVES HIS CHURCH

Christ loved the church and gave himself up for her, that he might sanctify
her, having cleansed her by the washing of water with the word, so that
he might present the church to himself in splendor. (Eph. 5:25–27)

What's something you've learned to love because someone you love
also loves it? Maybe you never cared for coffee until your fiancée told
you she wanted to spend every Saturday morning for the rest of her life
drinking coffee together on your front porch—and now, twenty years
later, your home has more machines to brew coffee than you could use
in a month of Saturdays. Or maybe it's your love for dogs or camping
or modern art that has been ignited solely because your friend or son
loves them. Things you never thought twice about are now precious
to you because someone you cared about showed you their value.

There's not much about the church that would naturally incline
us to love it. An unimpressive group of people with off-key voices
and awkward habits doesn't automatically stir up devotion. And when
we are hurt, we are even less likely to overflow with affection for
the congregation on Sundays. But today's verses give us a powerful
reason to keep showing up: Jesus loves the church.

As Ephesians 5 explains, the grand goal of Christ's redeeming
work is his church. Although he already knew every sin of every
person in his church—every foolish word, harmful act, rebellious
thought, and impure desire—he still became man on their behalf.
And "having loved his own who were in the world, he loved them
to the end" (John 13:1). Even when his people's sins inflicted on him
the greatest harm that has ever been done, Christ overflowed in love.
Christ lived a perfect life, was crucified and buried, and rose again—all
so that he could gather his people into his church.

Furthermore, he continues to be intimately concerned with the well-being of his church—providing the Word and Spirit for her sanctification and cleansing. Every Sunday, when God's people meet together as the dwelling place of the Spirit (1 Cor. 3:16) to receive his Word read and sung and preached and prayed, Christ demonstrates his ongoing love for us. And he promises to tenderly care for his church until that day when he "present[s] the church to himself in splendor" (Eph. 5:27).

After conflict, neglect, or disappointment in the church, we need this truth. In today's verses, and throughout all of the Scripture, the Lord affirms that he loves his people so much that he would even send the Son to die for them. The church we belong to is "the church of God, which he obtained with his own blood" (Acts 20:28). Although right now we may not be able to see anything beautiful about the people with whom we worship, Christ declares them lovely.

> **Read.** Read 1 John 4:7–21. What does God command in these verses? What are some of the reasons given why we should love one another in the church? It might seem impossible to try to love the church, especially when you've been hurt. How does it encourage you to know that God's love abides in you by his Spirit?
>
> **Reflect.** What is something you've grown to love because of someone else? Pastor Jeremy Walker wrote, "It is like God to love those whom God loves—it is godliness." Have you ever thought of loving the church as essential to godliness?
>
> **Pray.** Tell the Lord about ways that your love for the church has shriveled. Thank him for Christ's abundant love for you and for everyone who belongs to him. Ask him to send his Spirit to cultivate love for the church in your heart.

DAY 30

CHRIST UNITES HIS CHURCH

I do not ask for these only, but also for those who will believe in me
through their word, that they may all be one, just as you, Father,
are in me, and I in you, that they also may be in us, so that the
world may believe that you have sent me. (John 17:20–21)

During his earthly ministry, Jesus witnessed discord and division among his disciples. We might expect that living with Jesus and listening daily to his teaching would have made them a completely peaceful group. But the Twelve argued with each other over who was the greatest (Mark 9:33–34) and over who would attain places of honor in his kingdom (Matt. 20:20–24). One of his disciples even left the others in order to betray him (John 18:1–11).

Our greatest hurts in the church can come when we experience division and conflict in the congregation—when friends disagree, righteous people part ways, and members of the same body take sides against each other. Knowing this, in John 17 Jesus prayed for unity for his church. In today's verses we read the words of Jesus's high-priestly prayer, the prayer he offered just before his arrest and crucifixion. Having prayed for himself and for his disciples, Jesus then began to pray for the church that would soon grow from the disciples' gospel proclamation (v. 20). With these words, Jesus prayed for us.

He asked the Father to make his people one, even "perfectly one" (v. 23). The unity Christ pleads for is so complete that it parallels the unity between the persons of the Trinity (v. 22). Jesus didn't pray for surface-level politeness; he prayed for Godlike oneness.

And the prayers of the Son are always answered by the Father. Our sinless Savior prayed perfectly according to the will of the Father, and so we can trust that his prayers for unity will be answered. Any oneness we experience in this life is a reason to praise God and to look with hope for God to use it in the conversion of those around us (v. 21). And because of Christ's prayers and his work on the cross, the church's final unity is assured. The perfect Christ will have a perfect bride (Eph. 5:27), and the whole world will bow before him (Phil. 2:10).

Dear Christian, you can work for unity in the church with confidence—even if sometimes through tears—knowing Jesus is praying for you. Although you may not experience complete unity in any congregation in this life, you have every reason to pray for it yourself, to keep showing up expecting it, and to look for its fullness in eternity. What the Son asks, the Father grants.

Read. Read Psalm 133. How does it encourage you to know that God delights in unity among his people? How do these verses give you boldness to pray for greater unity in your own church?

Reflect. Ephesians reminds us that "[Christ] himself is our peace" (2:14) and then calls us to be "eager to maintain the unity of the Spirit in the bond of peace" (4:3). How is it helpful to know that Christ is the one who actually accomplishes peace? What are some practical ways you can seek to maintain the God-wrought unity of your church?

Pray. Using the words of Psalm 133, ask the Lord to grant unity to your church. Praise him for being the God who can "command blessing." Tell him about ways division and conflict have brought sorrow to your congregation. Plead with him to send his Spirit and give your church "good and pleasant" unity. Thank him for being the source of life.

DAY 31

CHRIST DWELLS WITH
HIS CHURCH

I will not leave you as orphans; I will come to you. Yet a little while
and the world will see me no more, but you will see me. Because
I live, you also will live. In that day you will know that I am in
my Father, and you in me, and I in you. (John 14:18–20)

At some point, you've probably felt alone in church. Whether you
were sitting in a too-empty row of chairs or were surrounded by
people but experiencing hardship, you know what it's like to be
in a congregation and yet feel isolated. It can be difficult to keep
showing up.

In today's verses, Jesus prepared his disciples for the day when he
would no longer be bodily present on earth. He knew the believers
would be confused and saddened when he left to return to heaven,
and so he promised them he would always be present with his church
by his Spirit. The congregation of believers, Jesus says, is in him by
faith, and he is in us by his Spirit. Among the saints who are "in Christ"
(Eph. 1:1; Phil. 1:1; Col. 1:2; 1 Thess. 1:1; 2 Thess. 1:1), Jesus dwells.

Jesus's promise can encourage us when we feel alone in the
congregation. Most of us probably know that when we worship
together, we draw near to Christ. We petition him in prayer, praise
him in song, and exalt him in our confession of faith. We "enter his
gates with thanksgiving and his courts with praise" (Ps. 100:4). Even
better, the writer to the Hebrews tells us that we enter the heavenly
places and the very presence of Jesus (Heb. 12:18–24).

We draw near to Christ in worship, but what we may not realize is that he also draws near to us. Christ is always present with us,

wherever we are, but he especially promises his presence by his Spirit when we gather as the church (Matt. 18:20; 28:20). He is our preacher, proclaiming his Word to us; he is our worship leader, singing the songs of heaven alongside us (Heb. 2:11–13). Christ knows the worst about the sinners for whom he died, and yet he is not ashamed to call them brothers and sisters and to come close to them (Heb. 2:11). He promises to be in our midst, no matter how few or how bedraggled we are. The world doesn't recognize Christ's continued presence, but the church knows it intimately (John 14:19).

Hurtful situations in the church can strip away many aspects of church life that we once enjoyed. Conflicts diminish our fellowship within the community. Sin erodes our trust in church leaders. Personal sorrow clouds our joy in worship. Disappointments dampen our hope for the church's future. But these can't touch the most precious reality of life in the church: nothing can remove Christ from among his people.

When we come to worship with the church, Jesus will be there. And, on days when church hurts, this is a precious reason to keep showing up.

Read. Read Matthew 28:16–20. What is Jesus commissioning his church to do? In what ways might church members feel alone in this task? What is the encouragement he gives them? How does this comfort you today?

Reflect. Prophesying to a divided kingdom, Zephaniah foretold a day when God's people would hear: "The Lᴏʀᴅ your God is in your midst" (3:17). When our human relationships are hard, why is it particularly precious to know that God is near?

Pray. Tell the Lord about a time when you have felt alone in the church. Plead with him the promise of today's verse, asking him to draw near to you as you worship with his people.

DAY 32

CHRIST EXECUTES JUSTICE IN HIS CHURCH

*Do you not know that you are God's temple and that God's Spirit
dwells in you? If anyone destroys God's temple, God will destroy him.
For God's temple is holy, and you are that temple. (1 Cor. 3:16–17)*

One Sunday, my friend worshipped alongside beloved congregation members with whom she'd shared years of burdens and joys; the next Sunday, half the seats were empty and many of her friends were gone. She wept as she told me about later seeing those people in the grocery store or post office, not sure how to greet them. The situation was complex. The church's former pastor had promoted false doctrine and then encouraged people to leave the church with him. My friend was sad about her church family. She was angry at the pastor.

As people created in the image of a righteous and just God, we long for righteousness and justice to reign in the world and in his church. And when they don't seem to, we are rightly troubled.

Thankfully, as today's verses remind us, sin never goes unaddressed by God. Writing to a church that was divided, Paul called for gospel unity (1 Cor. 3:1–15). But if members persisted in fracturing the church, Paul warned that they would face God's justice.

First, Paul affirmed the church's value: "You are God's temple and . . . God's Spirit dwells in you." Then he declared that the penalty for harming the church would fit the crime: "If anyone destroys God's temple, God will destroy him." If someone sets a distant, abandoned building on fire, you'd be mildly concerned. If someone sets your house on fire, you'd be outraged. So it is with the Lord. The church is his dwelling, and anyone who damages it will be liable to judgment.

On the basis of God's promise, you can take your burden over sin in the church to him. You can be comforted that every such sin receives its due penalty. God has either laid it on Christ at the cross, or he will punish the sinner on the day of judgment. He will judge the careless and hurtful words spoken in back rooms and congregational meetings (Matt. 12:36). He will address church leaders whose example and teaching leads others to sin (Matt. 18:1–10). He will even adjudicate sinful *thoughts*—lust, partiality, envy, greed (Heb. 4:11–13). Every sinning church member will one day stand "naked and exposed" before Christ, required to "give account" (v. 13).

Dear Christian, you can seek a measure of justice in this life (through church discipline and, where appropriate, civil authorities), and you can trust God to bring complete justice in eternity. You can keep showing up, knowing that you may sometimes be sinned against in church, but also knowing that Christ guarantees justice.

> **Read.** Read Matthew 18:1–10. What does Jesus say about the value of believing children? What does he say about the punishment for those who would cause them to sin? Do these verses comfort you in your own situation? Why or why not?
>
> **Reflect.** Church discipline or censure (when the church takes official action to rebuke and address sin among its members) can be imperfect. It is, however, one significant way that Christ rules over his church and brings a measure of justice even in this life (Matt. 18:15–20; 1 Cor. 5:1–5). Why is it important to join a church that values and practices church discipline?
>
> **Pray.** Call out to the Lord. Tell him about the sin in your church that is hurting you and others. Ask him to grant justice in this life and in eternity. Plead with him the words of today's verses, reminding him of the church's value and his promise to punish those who would destroy it.

DAY 33

CHRIST PERFECTS
HIS CHURCH

Christ loved the church and gave himself up for her . . . so that he might present the church to himself in splendor, without spot or wrinkle or any such thing, that she might be holy and without blemish. (Eph. 5:25, 27)

Maybe you've heard the wry poem: "To live above, with saints we love, that will be glory. To live below, with saints we know, now that's a different story!" It may be a silly ditty, but it highlights the genuine disconnect we often feel between our current experiences and our vision of the church in eternity. Compared with the gathering in heaven, church on earth feels pretty rough. It might seem easier not to think about the future at all.

In today's verses, however, Paul encourages us to meditate on what's next for the church. First, we see that the church is so important to Christ that he gave himself up for her. As we noted on day 29, Christ left his place in heaven to take on human flesh and die the painful and shameful death of the cross for the sake of his church. What's more, says Paul, his sacrifice was not in vain. Christ did all of this with a grand goal in mind: the church's perfection. One day, because of his work on the cross and through his Word and Spirit, his gathered people will be sinless, strong, mature, and beautiful (see Eph. 4:11–16).

"Weeping may tarry for the night, but joy comes with the morning," writes the psalmist (30:5), and this is our hope in the church. The sorrows of life in the church are momentary, but the perfection of the church is certain and eternal. Little by little now, and completely one day soon, every wrong will be righted, every loss restored, and every division healed.

Although our experience of the church is often accompanied by hurt, we can trust the Lord's promise that he is at work sanctifying his church today and that he will make his church perfect in the end. We keep showing up because we know that what we have now is not all there is to experience. Like the smiling wedding guest who exclaims to the bride, "I remember when you were still in diapers!" we will one day have an opportunity to celebrate firsthand just how far Christ's church has come.

Read. Read Revelation 7:9–12. God showed John the church's future in order to strengthen churches that were scattered, persecuted, and struggling. In his vision, John saw a church that is immense and diverse (v. 9). How can that encourage you when your church seems small or ineffective? John saw a church gathered in the near presence of the Lord (v. 9). How can that encourage you when your church seems apathetic or immature? John saw a church that boldly and harmoniously worships (vv. 10–12). How can that encourage you when your church seems ineffective or divided?

Reflect. Do you enjoy home makeover shows? Are you interested in "before" and "after" pictures of hairstyles or weight loss? Does it make you happy to have rooted for a team no one else expected to win? Most of us love a surprising transformation. Today, spend time meditating on the glorious future of the church, and allow Christ's promise of radical transformation to delight your heart as you participate in the church on earth.

Pray. Praise God for ruling over his church and for loving his church. Thank him for sending Christ to make his church holy. Using the words of today's verses, ask him to work in your congregation: erasing spots, smoothing wrinkles, healing blemishes. Ask him to encourage you now with thoughts of the church's perfect future.

WHAT HAVE OTHERS DONE IN MY SITUATION?

In this section, we're going to revisit the seven people or groups from the Bible whom we met in the first section. Paul, David, Anna, the Philippians, the returned exiles, Hannah, and even Jesus had stories like ours—stories of experiencing hurt in the assembly of believers. But thankfully, these hardships were not the end of their church stories, and your hardship doesn't have to be the end of yours. These individuals all found a way forward in the covenant community: Paul opened his heart after hurt, Anna kept her aging eyes on the Messiah, and Hannah sacrificially invested in a better future for God's people. Although none of them received a tidy solution to their past hurt, all of them went on to bear fruit and flourish.

I wrote these final meditations to encourage you that God can and does bring good from hard experiences. Jesus comes to his church "to comfort all who mourn; to grant to those who mourn in Zion—to give them a beautiful headdress instead of ashes, the oil of gladness instead of mourning, the garment of praise instead of a faint spirit; that they may be called oaks of righteousness, the planting of the LORD, that he may be glorified" (Isa. 61:2–3). All of the people in this section testify with their lives to the truth of this promise.

And if the Lord was gracious to them, he will also be gracious to you.

DAY 34

PAUL OPENED HIS HEART

Our heart is wide open. You are not restricted by us, but you
are restricted in your own affections. In return (I speak as
to children) widen your hearts also. (2 Cor. 6:11–13)

As a young adult, I volunteered to help with my church's women's retreat. The committee put me in charge of organizing and serving breakfast for the event. I'd never had that much responsibility before, and I took it seriously. The first morning, I eagerly headed for the meeting room and began laying out the coffee and treats I purchased. To my eyes, everything looked perfect. But when I ducked into the kitchen for the cream and sugar, I overheard women in the other room complaining about the breakfast. Tears blurred my vision. I wanted to stay in that kitchen and never come out.

When we are hurt in the church, it can be hard to see a way forward. Our instinct is to withdraw, protect ourselves, and avoid the potential for additional hurt. We plan on skipping services or side-stepping congregation members in the hallways from now on. The only possibility appears to be hunkering down and never coming out.

But today's verses give us a glimpse of another, more hopeful, way.

As we saw on day 1, Paul experienced significant hurt in the church. When he was imprisoned for the sake of the gospel, no one stood with him and all the church members deserted him (2 Tim. 4:16). Elsewhere in the New Testament, we read about how Paul was rebuffed by church leaders (Acts 9:26), criticized by false teachers and their followers (2 Cor. 10:10), misrepresented by church members (2 Peter 3:16), and neglected by self-centered Christians (Phil. 2:21). We might assume withdrawal from the church—whether physically or emotionally—would be his next step.

But Paul didn't choose retreat. He chose to open the door of his heart. Paul knew that the Corinthians' problems were their problems: "You are not restricted by us." The sin in their hearts, their human weakness, and the wiles of Satan had all conspired to shrivel their love toward Paul. None of that was Paul's fault. In our own circumstances too, we can acknowledge that other people's sin is their own responsibility, and we can remember that their sin doesn't have the right to dictate our response.

Rather than imitating the restricted Corinthians, Paul lifted his eyes to a better model, imitating Christ himself, who "loved us and gave himself up for us" (Eph. 5:1–2). Whatever Satan's schemes or sinners' intentions, an experience of hurt doesn't have the power to close us off from the way of love in the church. Christ has set us free. Like Paul, we can look for the Spirit to "widen [our] hearts" toward his people and to help us demonstrate tender affection for them.

Read. Read Ephesians 5:1–2. How did Christ demonstrate love? How does being "beloved children" (v. 1) enable us to "walk in love" (v. 2), even toward those who have wronged us?

Reflect. Earlier in 2 Corinthians, Paul says, "I wrote to you out of much affliction and anguish of heart and with many tears, not to cause you pain but to let you know the abundant love that I have for you" (2:4). In the midst of affliction, Paul acted in love. Plan one loving thing you could do for someone who has hurt you. It could be as simple as praying for him or her or making an effort to say hello when you next meet.

Pray. Using the words of today's verse, ask the Lord to open your heart and enable you to walk in love.

DAVID CHOSE TO FORGIVE

And the king said to Shimei, "You shall not die." And
the king gave him his oath. (2 Sam. 19:23)

When David was at an extremely low point in his life, a member of the covenant community attacked him—literally. Shimei, a man from Saul's household, came out to meet David; he "cursed continually" (2 Sam. 16:5) and "threw stones at David" and at everyone who was with him (v. 6). In the hearing of David's servants and soldiers, Shimei called the king a "worthless man" (v. 7) and taunted him about his rebellious son, Absalom (v. 8).

Immediately, David's companion Abishai asked to kill Shimei for his insolence, but David stayed his hand. He entrusted himself to the Lord: either God had told Shimei to curse him or God would curse Shimei (vv. 10–12). Later, Shimei came out to meet David again. This time, Shimei asked for mercy. Again, Abishai urged vengeance. And again, with the words of today's verse, David stayed his hand. Twice, David had the opportunity to kill Shimei, and twice he chose to forgive.

David's response to Shimei and also his psalm of anguish over the friend who wounded him (Ps. 55, see day 2), rest on a God who is sovereign and loving. David didn't understand why these hardships came to him, yet he knew that God would do what was best. He cast himself on a God who listens to his people (55:1, 17), saves the weak (vv. 16, 18), sustains the righteous (v. 22), and brings justice (vv. 9, 19; 2 Sam. 16:10–12). When we, likewise, have been sinned against, we can say with David, "But I will trust in you" (Ps. 55:23).

This, in turn, allows us to extend forgiveness to those who have sinned against us. Because we believe that God's justice and mercy will be rightly administered—"the LORD will look on the wrong done to me, and . . . the LORD will repay me with good for his cursing" (2 Sam. 16:12)—we can ask for God's help to overlook the offenses that have come against us. When someone has gossiped about us, when church members walk out in anger, when the pastor ignores a request for help, we can leave it with the Lord, knowing that he sees. We can refuse to hold that sin against the person, knowing God will deal justly. We can step freely into the future, trusting God will do what is right.

In this, we imitate our Lord Jesus, about whom Peter tells us, "When he was reviled, he did not revile in return; when he suffered, he did not threaten, but continued entrusting himself to him who judges justly" (1 Peter 2:23). On the cross, Jesus could say, "Father, forgive them" (Luke 23:34) because he rested on God's sovereign goodness.

If God is trustworthy—and he is!—we, like David and Jesus, can choose to forgive.

Read. Read Luke 23:32–38. List the sins that were committed against Jesus in this passage. What was Jesus's response? How might God be calling you to imitate Jesus in your current situation?

Reflect. Tim Keller defines forgiveness as "a promise *not* to exact the price of sin from the person who hurt you." What, then, are the implications of forgiveness for our thoughts, words, and actions toward the other person?

Pray. Praise the Lord for being a God who judges justly. Ask him to do what is best in your church situation. Ask for the help of his Spirit to forgive those who have sinned against you. Thank him for forgiving you all your sins.

DAY 36

ANNA CONTINUED
TO WORSHIP

*She did not depart from the temple, worshiping with fasting
and prayer night and day. And coming up at that very hour she
began to give thanks to God and to speak of him to all who were
waiting for the redemption of Jerusalem. (Luke 2:37–38)*

Often the thing we most want to do when church hurts is to stop showing up. Sunday becomes the hardest day of the week, and it feels easier—and safer—to stay home. If we don't engage, we can't get hurt. If we don't try, we won't be disappointed. If we don't go, we can't be ignored.

As we saw on day 3, Anna had many reasons to stay away from worship. Because she lived in a fallen world, her husband had died and her own body was wasting away. Because she lived among sinners, she was vulnerable. Because Satan prowled, she faced temptations to discouragement.

Anna could have allowed these circumstances to cut her off from the place of God's promised presence, but she didn't. As a faithful Jew, she would have known the words of Malachi: "The Lord whom you seek will suddenly come to his temple" (3:1). Anna knew that the Messiah was going to show up in the temple, and so she didn't let anything keep her from showing up there too. Night and day, with fasting and prayer, over months and years, she continued to worship the Lord exactly where he said he would be.

Then, "coming up at that very hour," Anna saw Jesus. To unspiritual eyes, the baby didn't look much like a savior or a king, but to the eyes of the elderly woman who had already been worshipping him for decades, he looked like a promise fulfilled. Joyfully, she announced his arrival to all the faithful. In that moment in the temple, Anna was still old. She was still a widow. She was still vulnerable. But she was not alone.

We too have the Lord's promise that he will be present by his Spirit when we worship with his congregation: "Where two or three are gathered in my name, there am I among them" (Matt. 18:20). Although the actions of sinners and the devices of Satan might be significant obstacles as we consider going to worship, they can't nullify this promise or bar us from drawing near to Christ.

Whatever our individual circumstances, corporate worship is always an act of resistance. In every pew sits a person whom Christ has rescued from the clutches of hell and redeemed for his glory. What's more, each worshipper has defied Satan's entrapments and sin's discouragements that very day in order to come into God's presence with praise. Like Anna, each of us shows up to worship against the world's odds. And Christ—who triumphed over evil on our behalf—meets us there.

> **Read.** Read Luke 18:1–8. What did the widow do? What did the judge do? How is God like the judge in this passage? How is he different? Why does Jesus say he told this parable? How can this parable encourage you to continue approaching God in worship even when church hurts?
>
> **Reflect.** Why might Satan want to keep you from worship and from being in Christ's presence? How does recognizing his evil intent help you to withstand his tactics?
>
> **Pray.** Tell the Lord about a time when you wanted to stop going to church to worship. Ask him to give you the spirit of Anna, who "did not depart" from the place of worship. Thank him for promising to meet with his people when they gather (Matt. 18:20). Look expectantly for Christ's presence the next time you are in church.

DAY 37

PHILIPPIAN BELIEVERS PURSUED RECONCILIATION

Yes, I ask you also, true companion, help these women, who have labored
side by side with me in the gospel together with Clement and the rest
of my fellow workers, whose names are in the book of life. (Phil. 4:3)

Following the terrorist attacks on September 11, 2001, the New York
Metropolitan Transportation Authority debuted a new public aware-
ness slogan: "If You See Something, Say Something." The Authority
knew that people (especially New Yorkers!) prefer to mind their own
business and not get involved in unfamiliar situations. But intervening
by alerting the proper authorities can save lives.

The people in Philippi may have wanted to avoid saying something too. As we saw on day 4, Euodia and Syntyche were arguing
with each other and the whole church knew about it. The congregation members may have wanted to trust that the two women would
sort it out on their own. Or they may have assumed the situation was
hopeless. But Paul knew the women needed help. He called on the
Philippian pastor ("I ask you . . . help these women," v. 3), and, by
publicly announcing the plan, he encouraged the entire congregation
to support their reconciliation.

In times of church conflict, it can seem easier not to get involved.
We may naively hope the situation will resolve on its own or assume
it never will. We may be reluctant to seem nosy by asking a pastor to
help, or we may be so hurt by the things we've witnessed that we're
reluctant to wade in again. In any case, keeping our distance (or leaving the church entirely) presents an attractive option.

But the disunity of arguing church members doesn't have the power to push us away from the church. Although Satan would love to isolate us by multiplying the evil effects of a single argument, Christ came to be our peace (Eph. 2:14). In the power of his Spirit, and as far as it depends on us, we seek to "live peaceably with all" (Rom. 12:18). Even when other believers are acting foolishly, we can commit to showing up with grace and a readiness to forgive. And, rather than walking past, we can help others do the same.

When conflicts arise in the church, we can foster peace. Our first recourse is prayer—seeking the help of the reconciling God who delights when his people dwell in unity (Ps. 133). We can also promote unity by being careful with our own speech—saying only what is edifying and resisting Satan's attempts to draw us into foolish words. Depending on our relationship to the people in the conflict, we may also have opportunity to offer counsel—encouraging church members to repent and forgive, and walking the steps of resolution with them (Matt. 18:15–18).

Read. Read Matthew 18:15–20. What are the steps for addressing sin that Jesus lays out? What do these verses teach you about when it may be necessary for additional people to get involved in conflict resolution? How does it encourage you to know that Jesus promises his presence in this process (v. 20)?

Reflect. Write out the words of Matthew 18:20 and post the verse somewhere you will see it on Sunday morning before church: stick it on your bathroom mirror, put it next to your car keys, or tape it to the cover of your Bible. Resolve, by the Spirit's help, to promote peace and reconciliation wherever you can, and take comfort from Christ's promised presence.

Pray. Tell the Lord about the disunity in your church. Ask him to grant peace. Ask him to equip you to help. Thank him for being the peace we need (Eph. 2:14).

DAY 38

RETURNED EXILES
KEPT SERVING

But Zerubbabel, Jeshua, and the rest of the heads of fathers' houses
in Israel said to them, "You have nothing to do with us in building a
house to our God; but we alone will build to the LORD, the God of Israel,
as King Cyrus the king of Persia has commanded us." (Ezra 4:3)

The returned exiles, as we saw on day 5, were grieving. Having
worshipped in the first temple, the old men wept at the smallness
of the second (Ezra 3:12–13). The ark was gone, the people were
diminished in number, and their place of worship was a shadow of
its former glory. The future looked bleak. What's more, enemies
of God's people tried to deceive them and then to discourage them
(4:1–2, 4–5). It's not hard to imagine the old men considering whether
they should just give up.

In today's verses, however, the men rallied. They remembered the
purpose of the temple ("a house to our God"), the goal of their con-
struction labors ("to the LORD, the God of Israel"), and their unique
calling to do the work ("we alone will build . . . as . . . the king . . . has
commanded us"). They refused to let the wicked schemes of others
or the outward insignificance of their task keep them from working
for God's glory in the place of worship, one cedar plank at a time.

When the situation in our own churches is discouraging, we can
resist the temptation to give up and instead find ways to serve God.
When a beloved pastor moves on, we can look for opportunities to
encourage his replacement. When a favorite ministry ceases to exist,
we can offer to help with a different one. When fewer and fewer
people show up each Sunday, we can do the good work of praying

earnestly for the Lord to add to the number those who are being saved. In the face of hardship, there is still good work for the church to do in the world—"the harvest is plentiful," promised Jesus (Matt. 9:37)—and we have the privilege of persisting in it.

Laboring in the church after hurt is not easy; we often feel weak and our discouragement is great. But as we keep serving, we—like the returned exiles—will slowly rebuild what has been damaged. The Lord may use our labors to renew evangelistic efforts, restore relationships, or revive biblical commitment in the congregation. And even if our church never returns to its former glory, we will know we have served him. As Ezra reported about the faithful workers, "the eye of their God was on [them]" (Ezra 5:5).

Read. Read Romans 16. What are some ways the people in this list served Paul and the church? How did serving alongside these people foster Paul's love for them? How have you seen service create similar bonds of love? As you keep serving in your church, how can it encourage you that the Lord tenderly records each of these people's names and their work in his Word?

Reflect. Elisabeth Elliot, widow of Jim Elliot and missionary to the Waorani people of Ecuador, said, "I don't know any more comforting motto in my life—and it has become a life motto for me—than these words, 'Do the next thing.'" Through loss, grief, and hardship, Elliot encouraged her heart that the Lord always had something—however small—for her to do for his glory. What might be the "next thing" the Lord would have you do in your church this week?

Pray. Tell the Lord about the discouragements that you face in your church. Ask him to help you to remember the purpose of serving in the church: his glory. Ask him to give you strength to continue to serve.

DAY 39

HANNAH DECIDED
TO COMMIT

For this child I prayed, and the LORD has granted me my petition
that I made to him. Therefore I have lent him to the LORD. As
long as he lives, he is lent to the LORD. (1 Sam. 1:27–28)

Hannah, as we saw on day 6, had been badly mistreated by the man who was supposed to provide spiritual care for her and the rest of the congregation. Eli ignored her needs and falsely accused her, and he allowed his sons to use their own leadership positions to corrupt corporate worship and harm God's people (1 Sam. 1:9–18; 2:12–17; 2:22–25). Eli was both sinful and weak, and his actions received their just consequences. But "the LORD remembered" Hannah and gave her the child she prayed for (1:19).

Holding the infant Samuel in her arms, Hannah had a choice. She could allow her leader's failures to keep her from worshipping the Lord and beholding his redemptive work among his people, or she could press on. Ultimately, Hannah's love for the Lord compelled her. She knew his goodness and power, she rested in his justice, and she trusted his promises (see 1 Sam. 2:1–10). Most of all, Hannah believed God would one day send his perfect anointed King to lead his people (v. 10)—and she decided to pursue the good of his kingdom until he did.

For Hannah, committing to God's redeeming work meant giving up her only son so he could be a better spiritual leader than Eli and his sons were. She took young Samuel to Shiloh, and she left him there to become a priest (1 Sam. 1:24–28). She knew God's people were precious to him and so she willingly—and radically—sacrificed for their good. In this, she foretold the work of God himself who "did

89

not spare his own Son but gave him up for us all" (Rom. 8:32), sending Jesus to be the Good Shepherd who rescues his people from the clutches of destructive shepherds and gathers them into one healthy flock (Jer. 23:1–6; John 10:11–16).

We too have a choice. Having been hurt by weak or sinful leaders, we can walk away and allow their conduct to cut us off from the church's future. But Hannah—and the Lord—shows us another possibility. We can commit. Whether we stay in one congregation or join another, we can rejoice that the Father gave up his Son for his people. We can trust that King Jesus is advancing his kingdom in the church, and we can sacrifice for its good. We can even, like Hannah, believe so strongly in the future of God's people that we raise our children to love the church and to desire to serve in it.

Year after year, as Hannah returned to Shiloh with clothes for Samuel, she reaffirmed her decision to hope in the Lord and invest in his people's good (1 Sam. 2:18–21). In this, she points us to a way forward.

Read. Read 1 Samuel 2:1–10. Which phrases reveal Hannah's confidence in God's goodness, power, and justice? Where does she express her hope for the future? How does knowing God's character help you commit to the future of his kingdom in the church?

Reflect. If you knew one day your team would win a championship, your department a big contract, or your music group a show at a major venue, how would that encourage you to sacrifice today? How does the guaranteed future of the church motivate you to invest in it this week?

Pray. Using words from Hannah's prayer (1 Sam. 2:1–10), thank God for his goodness and power, praise him for his justice, and ask him to send his King to take up his visible reign. Ask the Lord to give you a heart that exults in him and works for the good of his kingdom until his return.

DAY 40

JESUS LOOKED TO ETERNITY

*And I saw the holy city, new Jerusalem, coming down out of heaven
from God, prepared as a bride adorned for her husband. And
I heard a loud voice from the throne saying, "Behold, the dwelling
place of God is with man. He will dwell with them, and they will
be his people, and God himself will be with them as their God.
He will wipe away every tear from their eyes, and death shall be
no more, neither shall there be mourning, nor crying, nor pain
anymore, for the former things have passed away." (Rev. 21:2–4)*

The longer I've been in the church, the more I've realized church is
hard at times for everyone. Walking into the sanctuary on Sunday
morning, I join an assembly of struggling people. The woman to my
right who attends worship over the objections of her unbelieving
husband. The man on my left whose young adult child was excom-
municated. The family whose previous pastor engaged in scandalous
sin and who are still wary. The single person who feels overlooked and
neglected; the mother of four who feels overlooked and neglected.
The teenager who wishes the youth group were bigger, like it used to
be. Even the pastor, who knows his sermon will be met with critical
comments—or complete indifference—at the door.

Our reasons for sighing on Sunday are diverse, but in one way or
another we all know what it feels like to hurt in church. So does Jesus.
As we saw on day 7, Christ experienced mistreatment, abandonment,
and little fruit—even among his closest followers. The troubles and
temptations that have come to us also came to him (Heb. 4:15). And yet,
as we have seen throughout this book, he continues to love his church.

How did Jesus have the strength to endure suffering on behalf
of the church? He was looking to the church's future. The writer to

the Hebrews tells us that Jesus "for the joy that was set before him endured the cross, despising the shame" (Heb. 12:2). Jesus trusted the Father and believed that the church's future would be joyful. By thinking much of eternity, he was able to think little of his suffering (see 2 Cor. 4:17–18).

In today's verses, the Lord graciously gives us a glimpse of the church in eternity so that we too can set our eyes on that final day when the church will be a place of untarnished joy and worship. In that day, no one will sin against us and we will sin against no one. In that day, our Lord will set all wrongs right and heal all wounds. In that day, our weaknesses will be turned to strength and our blemishes to beauty. And in that day, we will dwell together with our God forever.

Dear hurting Christian, take heart.

Read. Read Psalm 22:19–31. Jesus took this psalm on his lips as he was suffering on the cross for the sake of the church (Matt. 27:46; Mark 15:34). What are some of the metaphors for hardship (vv. 20–21)? What are some of the images of the congregation and Christ's place in it (vv. 22–31)? How do you think this vision of the church's future gave Jesus strength in his final earthly hours? How can it give you strength in your current trouble?

Reflect. How does knowing that church is hard in some way for everyone give you sympathy for the people in your congregation? How can each person's example of overcoming obstacles to show up on Sunday be an encouragement to the others?

Pray. Praise God for one thing you've learned about him in this book. Ask him for help to put into practice one thing you've realized you need to do. As you did on day 1, thank him for having his eyes toward you and his ears toward your cry (Ps. 34:15).

ACKNOWLEDGMENTS

This book began over breakfast around a table in New Hampshire. Overlooking a lake at a Christian conference center, I asked the question, "What are the reasons why church can hurt?" and, between bites of eggs and waffles, my friends (and fellow church members) started a list. Every item on the list had a story attached to it, whether a personal story or a story they'd heard from a friend. These were the first ripples in the water. Over the next months, I asked more people the same question, and I heard their stories too. Others came along and read outlines and sections and chapters, giving me invaluable feedback about my work. Some even read the entire manuscript. The weaknesses in these pages are mine. The strengths are because of their help.

Thanks be to God
    for Dave who asked me to write a book on church hurt,
    for Amanda who held my hand until I wrestled an outline and a title onto the page,
    for Kristy, Christina, Sue, and Rachel, who came to New Hampshire with me,
    for Nate and Lindsey, Chris and Emily, and Gabe and Jennifer, who continued the conversation,
    for Kathy, Winfree, Rachel, Rob, Jared, and Dad, who fixed my theological errors and unsplit my infinitives,
    for my husband, Rob, who brought me lattes and reminded me of the main point, and who makes everything better,

for my children, Brad, Caleb, Nate, and Evie, who give me joy,

and for the people of West Springfield Covenant Community Church, who keep showing up.

A WORD ON BIBLICALLY
FAITHFUL CHURCHES

It's beyond the scope of this book to make the case for what constitutes a biblically faithful church, but that doesn't mean it's not an important question. For helpful resources on that subject, see *Nine Marks of a Healthy Church* by Mark Dever (revised ed., Wheaton, IL: Crossway, 2004); *The Church: Glorious Body, Radiant Bride* by Mark G. Johnston (Carlisle, PA: Banner of Truth, 2018); or my book *A Place to Belong: Learning to Love the Local Church* (Wheaton, IL: Crossway, 2020). Although these books express limited differences about sacraments and church government, they agree in the essentials of what a church ought to be. For a more exhaustive treatment, see the two-volume classic *The Church of Christ: A Treatise on the Nature, Powers, Ordinances, Discipline and Government of the Christian Church* by James Bannerman (1868, repr., Vestavia Hills, AL: Solid Ground, 2009). Reading these books, studying God's Word, and seeking the counsel of mature believers can help you identify a church where God will be glorified and your soul nourished.

HOW TO USE THIS
BOOK IN A GROUP

Church hurt is often a personal and even private sorrow. The hard situations you've encountered in church may be experiences you've voiced only to the Lord. This book was written to minister to you in those secret places. But church hurt is also a common struggle. Although the believers you know may not have had exactly the same troubles as you have, they've probably walked through hard things at church too. It may be helpful for you to open the Scriptures together, encourage one another, and ask the Holy Spirit to comfort and direct you. What you've read in these pages can be a resource as you do.

Gathering a Group

Who are the believers in your life who want to apply God's Word to their difficult church situation? These may be fellow congregation members who have recently walked through the same trial (a congregational split, a pastor's moral failing, a struggling church plant), or they may be part of a church small group or study group that wants to understand various church hurts. Alternatively, a mature believer could use this book to mentor you one-on-one.

Establishing Group Rules

From the beginning, make it clear that your group is committed to four things:

- pursuing love for God
- focusing on God's Word
- caring for one another
- practicing righteousness

Your goal for your group is that each member would grow in love for the Lord who first loved us. Some group members may show up questioning God's goodness or righteousness; your group should acknowledge these common doubts while unapologetically pursuing a deeper relationship with him. To that end, your meeting time will center on God's Word—the place where God reveals himself. It may be tempting to spend most of your discussion rehearsing the details of each person's hurt, but it will be more helpful to focus together on Scripture and allow its universal truths to shape everyone's understanding of their experience. Group members should also agree to do good to one another. This means you'll speak truthfully and kindly to each other, point one another to the Lord's comfort, and keep group discussions confidential. You'll build relationships with one another marked by love and trust, while gently helping one another fight temptation to sins like bitterness and slander. Finally, your group must commit to doing what's right even when it's uncomfortable— for example, if someone in the group discloses a crime against him or her, the group must report it to the proper authorities.

Organizing Your Discussion

This book is divided into six sections, and those sections can provide the topics for six group meetings. Between meetings, group members can read the meditations in that section on their own. When you come together, you can select one or more of the "Read" prompts to follow together. Additionally, you can choose one or more of the "Reflect" questions to help you apply the truth of God's Word to your own situation.

Praying Together

In any hard experience, what we need most is God's help. Designate a significant portion of your meeting time to prayer. Use the "Pray" prompts to guide you—assign a different prompt to each person or choose one to focus your time on a single concern. Additionally, you can turn the Bible texts from the daily readings into prayer: praise God for his character revealed in those verses, confess ways his Word has exposed your sin, ask God to do what he's promised, and intercede for those who have the needs described.

NOTES

4 Lifeway Research study results: Lifeway, "Some Losses Inevitable, but Church Can Guard the Back Door," *Lifeway Research*, Oct. 26, 2006, https://research.lifeway.com/2006/10/26/some-losses-inevitable-but-churches-can-guard-the-back-door/.

7 most people believed the family line extinct: William Hendriksen, *Luke*, New Testament Commentary (Grand Rapids: Baker Book House, 1978), 171.

30 "God is always doing 10,000 things": Quoted by Desiring God (@desiringGod), Twitter, November 8, 2012, 11:56 a.m., https://twitter.com/desiringgod/status/266584993881550849?lang+en.

42 "Sin gives Satan a power over us": Thomas Brooks, *Precious Remedies against Satan's Devices* (Carlisle, PA: Banner of Truth Trust, 1652, repr. 2000), 33.

45 "Satan . . . being fallen from light": Brooks, 15.

45 "be frequent in comparing themselves": Brooks, 89.

46 "quick-sighted abroad": Brooks, 89.

56 getting help outside the congregation: I'm talking here about asking other believers for wisdom about how to proceed in a church situation, but if your situation involves criminal behavior (such as abuse), you will also need to take it to the appropriate civil authorities.

68 "It is like God to love": Jeremy Walker, *Life in Christ: Becoming and Being a Disciple of the Lord Jesus Christ* (Grand Rapids: Reformation Heritage, 2013), 104.

81 David chose to forgive Shimei twice: At his reign's end, David turned Shimei over to Solomon's judgment and even authorized his son to kill Shimei. Following David's death, Solomon first placed Shimei under house arrest, but when Shimei broke the terms, Solomon had him killed (1 Kings 2:8–9, 36–46). Some commentators believe David acted righteously until the end in regard to Shimei and was merely telling Solomon to keep a close eye on someone who had proved to be traitorous in the past. Forgiving someone doesn't mean we are naive about that person's potential for future sin. Others believe David sinned in his instructions to Solomon and duplicitously went back on his word of pardon to Shimei. It's difficult to know how to understand this final chapter in the story of David and Shimei, but we do know that not every action of every person in the Bible is exemplary and even their failures point us to Christ—the better King who never fails to act with perfect justice and perfect forgiveness.

82 "a promise not to exact the price": Timothy Keller, *Forgive: Why Should I and How Can I?* (New York: Viking, 2022), 173.

85 "If You See Something, Say Something" campaign: Department of Homeland Security, "About the Campaign," March 21, 2023. https://www.dhs.gov/see-something-say-something/about-campaign.

88 "I don't know any more comforting motto": Elisabeth Elliot, *Gateway to Joy* broadcast, "Do the Next Thing: Really Only One Thing to Do," June 19, 1991. https://elisabethelliot.org/resource-library/gateway-to-joy/do-the-next-thing-really-only-one-thing-to-do/

From P&R and the
Biblical Counseling Coalition

PATIENCE

WAITING
WITH HOPE

31-DAY DEVOTIONALS FOR LIFE

MEGAN HILL

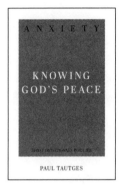

ANXIETY

KNOWING
GOD'S PEACE

31-DAY DEVOTIONALS FOR LIFE

PAUL TAUTGES

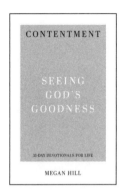

CONTENTMENT

SEEING
GOD'S
GOODNESS

31-DAY DEVOTIONALS FOR LIFE

MEGAN HILL

ANGER

CALMING
YOUR HEART

31-DAY DEVOTIONALS FOR LIFE

ROBERT D. JONES

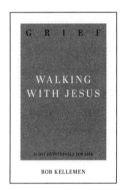

GRIEF

WALKING
WITH JESUS

31-DAY DEVOTIONALS FOR LIFE

BOB KELLEMEN

SHAME

BEING
KNOWN AND
LOVED

31-DAY DEVOTIONALS FOR LIFE

ESTHER LIU

In the 31-Day Devotionals for Life series, biblical counselors and Bible teachers guide you through Scripture passages that speak to specific situations or struggles, helping you to apply God's Word to your life in practical ways day after day.

Devotionals endorsed by Brad Bigney, Kevin Carson, Mark Dever, John Freeman, Gloria Furman, Melissa Kruger, Mark Shaw, Winston Smith, Joni Eareckson Tada, Ed Welch, and more!

Also by Megan Hill

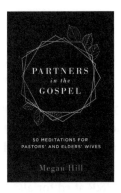

Focusing on the joys and challenges of the elder's wife's heart, home, church, and community, these fifty short devotional meditations will encourage and equip wives of church leaders.

"If you're the wife of a pastor or elder, let me encourage you: read this book. *Partners in the Gospel* is full of wisdom, insight, compassion, and perspective. These daily devotions by Megan Hill will remind you of the truth, offer you sympathy in your struggles, and refresh your heart as you walk alongside your husband in ministry."
—**Melissa Kruger**, pastor's wife

"I am glad to recommend Megan Hill's *Partners in the Gospel* to any woman whose husband is in ministry. Not only are its contents highly relatable, but its application is both challenging and encouraging. It will remind you of what is true, then help you to apply that truth to your everyday life."
—**Aileen Challies**, elder's wife